SPECIAL FORCES

Lt. Col. GEORGE FORTY, OBE, FMA

Airlife

England

Copyright © 2002 Airlife Publishing Ltd

First published in the UK in 2002
by Airlife Publishing Ltd

British Library Cataloguing-in-Publication Data
  A catalogue record for this book
  is available from the British Library

ISBN 1 84037 206 0

Typeset by Rowland Phototypesetting Ltd,
Bury St Edmunds, Suffolk.
Printed in Hong Kong

Airlife Publishing Ltd
101 Longden Road, Shrewsbury, SY3 9EB, England
E-mail: airlife@airlifebooks.com
Website: www.airlifebooks.com

Contents

Introduction

Elite military units are as old as the history of warfare itself; men like Alexander's Companions or the Persian Immortals were specialised shock troops who were only committed to battle when their special fighting abilities and weaponry were sufficient to turn the tables on the enemy. Other elite troops have, over the centuries, been used primarily as bodyguards for royalty or senior commanders, giving rise to some extraordinary 'elites' – such as the women of Emperor Nero's seraglio, whom he armed like Amazons with battleaxes and shields, intending to march at their head against the rebels during Galba's revolt!

However, it was the German storm-troopers of 1918, trained to infiltrate behind enemy lines, who were the true precursors of modern special forces. The division between special forces (SF) and elite forces has now become very blurred, so that the most recognisable types – the paratroopers and commandos, for example, as well as the more shadowy forces like the British SAS – are considered to be both 'special' and 'elite'. I have included examples of both, because all are undoubtedly among the most highly trained troops in the world.

Before discussing special forces, I must first explain the generally accepted meaning of the term 'special operations (SO)'. According to the United States Special Operations Forces Posture Statement 2000, these are actions which are conducted by specially organised, trained and equipped military or paramilitary forces in order to achieve military, political, economic or psychological objectives by unconventional means in hostile, denied or politically sensitive areas. They may be conducted in peacetime, in periods of conflict or during all-out war, independently or in co-ordination with conventional forces. The military and political situation frequently dictates such special operations, and such operations usually differ from conventional operations in their degree of risk, the operational techniques involved, their *modus operandi*, independence from friendly support and dependence upon essential operational intelligence, and the knowledge of the indigenous assets available.

This is an enormous subject to cover, so although I have tried to list as wide a selection of SF units as possible, I have deliberately confined the detailed explanations to certain of the more obvious units. However, I think it must be clear that the skills they have to acquire and the training methods used to acquire these skills do not differ to any marked degree between one country and another.

Acknowledgements

I have a great number of people and establishments to thank for their help with this book. First of all there are all the Defence Attaches in London to whom I initially wrote to make primary contact. Most were helpful and many gave me details of other more suitable contacts to approach in their home countries. From these I have obtained information and in some cases pictures. These contacts also gave me access to such major SF operators as the United States SOCCOM and its equivalents in various other countries (e.g. the UK). I must also thank individual press officers of HQ ARRC, HQ 16 Air Assault Brigade, Royal Marines, Stockholm Police, GSG9, KSK, Enzian, as well as the following picture sources: MPL, Patrick Allen, Avon Inflatables, Bofors, www.jantix.com, specialforces.net and Gilles Rivet/Concord Publications. In addition my sincere thanks go to Col David Eshel, late IDF, who wrote much of the Middle East section and provided many of the pictures. Despite all these invaluable sources I realise that there are still many gaps in this book, however, it is such a vast subject that it would be impossible to even list all the multitudinous SF units currently operating in various parts of the world. It certainly is a growth industry worldwide – and a very necessary one too, as the threats from global terrorism and international crime syndicates grow alarmingly quickly every year. I also fully appreciate that many of these SF units wish to maintain the cloak of secrecy that is so essential to some of their operations. The problem is that so many books have been written about them. For example, I have lost count of the number of books/videos, etc. about the British SAS, written by ex-members, that it is now extremely difficult for them to sensibly seek complete anonymity. However, all the material I have used in compiling the book has been unclassified and readily available.

Finally, I must thank my son, Jonathan, who has also researched and written much of the book. His expertise on the Internet has also been invaluable. Certainly his name should also appear on the cover, but like so many of the SF prefers to remain 'in the shadows'! I hope our efforts will be of interest.

GEORGE FORTY
Bryantspuddle

Abbreviations

AFCENT – Allied Forces Central Europe
ACE – Allied Command Europe
AFV – Armoured Fighting Vehicle
ARRC – Allied Rapid Reaction Corps
AWACS – Airborne Warning and Control System
BBE – *Bijzondere Bijstands Eenheid* (Netherlands)
CA – Civil Affairs
CIA – Central Intelligence Agency (USA)
CT – Counter-terrorism or combat team
DZ – Drop Zone
ETA – *Euzkadi ta Askatsuna* (Basque Nation and Liberty)
EOD – Emergency Ordnance Disposal
FSK – Fernspah Kompanie (Swiss)
GEO – *Gruppos Especiales de Operaciones* (Spain)
GIGN – *Group d'Intervention Gendarmerie Nationale* (France)
GIS – *Gruppo di Intervention Speciale* (Italy)
GPMG – General purpose machine-gun
GSG9 – *Grenzshutzgruppe 9* (Germany)
HAHO – High Altitude High Opening
HALO – High Altitude Low Opening
H&K – Heckler & Koch
IDF – Israeli Defence Forces
IS – Internal Security
LCM – Landing Craft Mechanised
LCT – Landing Craft Tank
LPD – Landing Platform Dock ship
LRRP – Long Range Reconnaissance Patrol
LST – Landing Ship Tank
MMG – Medium Machine-gun
NATO – North Atlantic Treaty Organisation
NCO – Non Commissioned Officer
OC – Officer Commanding
OP – Observation Post
QM – Quartermaster
PSYOP – Psychological Operations
REP – *Régiment Étranger de Parachutiste* (France)
RM – Royal Marines
SAS – Special Air Service
SBS – Special Boat Section
SCUBA – Self contained underwater breathing apparatus
SEAL – Sea, Air and Land
SF – Special Forces
SMG – Submachine-gun
SOF – Special Operations Forces
SOU – Special Operations Unit
SWAT – Special Weapons and Tactics
TA – Territorial Army
TALO – Tactical Air Landing Operations
USSOCOM – US Special Operations Command
2IC – Second in Command

NATO – ARRC

Although not by any means entirely composed of special forces, the NATO **immediate/rapid reaction forces** are immediately available to the Supreme Allied Commander, Europe (SACEUR) for crisis response and contain elite paratroop and commando units from many nations, together with some special forces units. They are thus multinational forces, held at a permanent state of readiness and allocated to major NATO commanders as authorised by the North Atlantic Council. They can be subdivided into:

- immediate reaction forces (IRF), capable of deployment within three to seven days
- rapid reaction forces (RRF), capable of deployment within seven to fifteen days

Allied Command Europe (ACE) Reaction Forces	
SACEUR	
Immediate Reaction Forces	Rapid Reaction Forces
IRF Air	RRF Air
ACE Mobile Force (Land)	Allied Rapid Reaction Corps
IRF Sea	RRF Sea

In close support to the air assault infantry battalions are HCR Scimitars and Chinook heavy lift helicopters – this one is lifting a Land Rover and a plastic fuel container. (Crown Copyright)

A patrol from the Pathfinder Platoon of HQ 16 Air Assault Brigade are seen here during a linked free-fall from a C-130 Hercules at 20,000 ft at the start of a HALO insertion. Breathing oxygen and carrying their M16A2 personal weapons strapped to their sides, they will free-fall to a predetermined altitude before breaking away and allowing their Hitefinder barometric opening devices to automatically deploy their GQ360 canopies.
(MPL International Ltd)

Both have employment options covering all regions of the Alliance. They can be employed on their own or as part of joint operations, for example in combination with one or more components of sea, land or air forces in combined operations or in combined joint operations with other NATO, national or international forces.

The concept for the **Allied Rapid Reaction Corps (ARRC)** was initiated in May 1991 and confirmed six months later. The concept calls for forces to meet any future challenge to NATO by providing SACEUR with a multinational corps, the forward elements of which can be ready to deploy in Western Europe within fourteen days. Currently ARRC trains for both peacekeeping and peacemaking tasks and encompasses servicemen from Belgium, Canada, Denmark, Germany, Greece, Italy, the Netherlands, Norway, Portugal, Spain, Turkey, the UK and the USA. Ten divisions are assigned to ARRC and any four could be placed under command for a particular operation. They range from armoured formations equipped with main battle tanks to light air-portable units which are more suited to difficult terrain, such as are found in the mountains or the Arctic.

The Allied Rapid Reaction Corps (ARRC) – Assigned Formations

Within the composition of the assigned ten divisions (see chart, page 8) there are a number of formations of special forces:

- one Belgian parachute commando brigade (four airborne infantry battalions)
- one German airborne brigade (31 Ab Bde containing three infantry battalions, one equipped with Wiesel light armoured tracked vehicles)
- one Netherlands air manoeuvre brigade (three airmobile infantry battalions and integral attack and transport helicopters)
- one Portuguese separate parachute brigade
- three Spanish brigades – one parachute, one airborne and one legion, forming the Spanish RRD (Rapid Reaction Division)
- one UK air assault brigade (16 Air Assault (UK) Bde)

These formations are covered in detail in their country of origin entry

It is also clear that in an emergency ARRC will be able to call on the SF of a number of committed nations, both large and small, that have not been shown in the chart. For example, within the divisional troops of the Multinational Division (Central) (MND(C)) there is a Dutch special forces company.

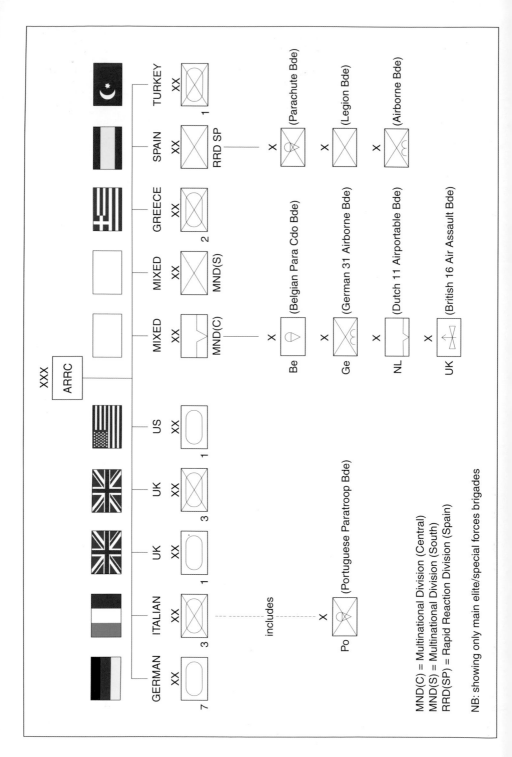

GERMAN   ITALIAN   UK   UK   US   XXX   MIXED   MIXED   GREECE   SPAIN   TURKEY

ARRC

XX 7   XX 3   XX 1   XX 3   XX 1   XX MND(C)   XX MND(S)   XX 2   XX RRD SP   XX 1

includes

X Po (Portuguese Paratroop Bde)

X Be (Belgian Para Cdo Bde)

X Ge (German 31 Airborne Bde)

X NL (Dutch 11 Airportable Bde)

X UK (British 16 Air Assault Bde)

X (Parachute Bde)

X (Legion Bde)

X (Airborne Bde)

MND(C) = Multinational Division (Central)
MND(S) = Multinational Division (South)
RRD(SP) = Rapid Reaction Division (Spain)

NB: showing only main elite/special forces brigades

The recently launched Landing Platform Helicopter (LPH) HMS Ocean which is for use in the Joint Rapid Deployment Force (JRDF) is seen here on her sea trials. She can take an entire Marine Commando of up to 850 men. (BAE Systems Marine)

Algeria

The first Algerian special force was the **19th Algerian Parachute Battalion** formed in January 1954 by the French Army. This was disbanded at Mortauban in France in July 1956. On its independence from France in July 1962 Algeria formed the first parachute commando battalion, followed later by two more. Training and equipment came from the Soviet Union. Between 1967 and 1969 one battalion was deployed to Fayid, Egypt, and elements took part in raids against the IDF during the War of Attrition across the Suez Canal.

At present there is a fully equipped airborne/special forces division in service.

Argentina

The history of the Argentine special forces began in the 1960s when a commando brigade, *Brigada del Ejercito 601*, was set up with American assistance, the training modelled along US Rangers lines. A little later another brigade, the **602nd**, was added, followed by the Navy *Agrupacion de Commandos Amphibios*, otherwise known as the *Buzos Tacticos*, a combat divers' commando company, and the most recent Air Force *Grupo de Operativa Especial de l'Armada* – long-range reconnaissance commandos. All these units accept only volunteers from other parts of the armed services with previous military experience. Following a three-day selection course successful survivors then complete a three-month course in close-quarters combat, and jungle and urban warfare, as well as navigation and survival courses at the Campo de Mayo Infantry School. All three service units are also parachute qualified at the Catamarca Airborne School and all took part in the 1982 Falklands War. The *Buzos Tacticos* were the first Argentine elements to land on the Islands, while the 601st fought with the British SAS for possession of Mount Kent (the high point overlooking Port Stanley), acquitting themselves very ably. They possess state-of-the-art equipment, including laser-sighted sniper rifles as well as the excellent FAL/FAP assault rifle.

Austria

Volunteers only are permitted to apply to join the Austrian **Commando Corps** (*Jagdkommando*) and they must have no previous convictions, be physically and mentally fit and prepared to do an additional six months voluntary military service on top of their normal national service. Aptitude testing requires both strength and courage and includes: a 24 km march in three and a half hours with a 10 kg pack and personal weapon, a dive from a 10 m tower, a thirty-minute non-stop swim, a 5 km run in twenty-four minutes and a suspended traverse along a 30 m sloping rope.

Commando training lasts for twenty-two weeks and takes place after basic military and preparatory cadre training. During their training the volunteers learn survival techniques, demolitions (some reaching Demolition Expert licence standard), parachuting (including free-fall parachuting), close-combat training (some under severe winter conditions), marksmanship, amphibious operations, alpine operations and first aid. They are also taught 'aid to the civil power', so that they are able to work with the civilian authorities and with other special forces such as the Austrian GEK Cobra, German GSG9 or American Delta Force, in hostage release situations and the like.

The main commando garrison is Wiener Neustadt, in Lower Austria, south of Vienna, where the Commando Centre is located.

RIGHT: *Roping down from a Bell helicopter.* (Austrian Armed Forces Photograph)

A squad of Austrian Jagdkommando practise storming a building, some in black Nomex, others in green, but all with body armour. (Austrian Armed Forces Photograph)

Australia

The first Australian SAS squadrons were raised during the Second World War to fight the Japanese behind their own lines, a difficult task which they accomplished with much *élan*. Following the war's end, like their British counterparts, they were briefly disbanded before being reformed in 1949. After three years of independence as **1st SAS Company** based at Swanbourne, in 1951 they were incorporated into the **Royal Australian Regiment (RAR)** as an airborne platoon. Then in 1957, again following the British pattern, they were given autonomy once more as **1st Special Air Service Company**. This unit evolved into a regiment-sized formation, the current **1st Special Air Service Regiment (SASR)**.

The prime special forces unit of the Australian armed forces today is the **Australian Special Air Service Regiment** (SASR). Its history is similar to that of the British SAS, with whom it has strong links, and stems from developments in special operations and counter-insurgency in the Cold War years, when ideological struggles were played out in low-level warfare that took place throughout several parts of the world. The need for a larger special forces capability led to the expansion of the 1st SAS Company into the Australian Special Air Service Regiment in September 1964, consisting of two Sabre squadrons. After intensive training both squadrons saw service in counter-insurgency and cross-border roles from February 1965 in Borneo to August 1966 in the Indonesian Confrontation working in conjunction with the British SAS. In 1962 members of the Australian SAS became part of the **Australian Army Training Team** working with US forces in Vietnam, with a third squadron being raised and sent to Vietnam in July 1966. Until 1971 each squadron then rotated, doing two tours each in Vietnam, where they soon established a reputation for tough and tenacious professionalism.

After Vietnam one squadron was disbanded, but a terrorist bomb attack on the Sydney Hilton Hotel on 13 February 1978 showed that Australia was vulnerable to terrorist attack. As a result some ten days later the SASR was formally designated the national counter-terrorist unit. Following this designation the TAG/OAT groups were soon organised (see box). Thus the SASR began to expand and in 1982 to help meet these new tasks the third Sabre squadron was reformed and another, the **Signals Squadron** (which attached a troop to each Sabre squadron), was raised. The TAG/OAT configurations also swiftly grew in size and resources. Since then, despite the inevitable cutbacks in defence expenditure by the Australian Government, the SASR has been consistently maintained. Recent operations have included the Gulf War, when one SASR squadron of 110 men joined with others from the New Zealand SAS to form the ANZAC SAS Squadron, deployed to Kuwait in February–May 1991, as part of a joint Allied force with British and US special forces.

The Land Rover Perentie 6x6 was specially developed in Australia to suit their conditions as a long-range patrol vehicle, which is longer (6 m), and heavier (4,840 kg), with a wider wheelbase (3.9 m) than the normal Land Rover. It is fitted with a machine-gun mount, a winch and two spare wheels. (Land Rover)

Based at Campbell Barracks, Swanbourne, the SASR has a strength of around 600 men, organised in six squadrons (three Sabre, one Base, one Operational Support and one Signals), along with a Regimental Headquarters (RHQ). The three Sabre squadrons operate a three-year cycle which gives them all the same capability. During the first, a development year, new volunteers are processed and the more experienced troopers attend advanced and specialist training courses. In the second year the squadron trains for its overt military responsibilities, including special operations in conventional theatres of war. In the third year training is geared towards covert operations. Base Squadron provides administrative and logistical support, while the Operational Support Squadron is responsible for specialist training and trials of new techniques and equipment. The specialised communications necessary for the regiment are provided by 152 Signals Squadron (SASR).

Selection and training is exceptionally rigorous and the initial selection course has an attrition rate of over 90 per cent. The very few who pass this stage then undertake a five-week familiarisation course, a four-week long-range patrol course and a three-week parachute course at Nowra, New South Wales. Later training continues to stress specialised development, including CT operations which provide a chance to develop other skills, such as those necessary to recruit and develop indigenous guerrilla allies in wartime. Completion of all training brings the coveted sand-coloured beret bearing the SAS badge.

The SASR works and trains in close liaison with US, British, and New Zealand special forces. More controversially, since 1992 there has also been considerable contact with the Indonesian special forces.

Uniforms and Equipment
SASR uniforms are identical to those of the Australian Army, with only the sand-coloured beret, cap badge and wings differentiating them from other standard units. Other special uniforms are worn according to the demands of particular operations. Equipment includes the normal range of Australian weapons and kit, but with some specialised items for specific roles. The usual rifle is either the M16A3 or the F88 Austeyr (locally manufactured version of the Steyr AUG). Other weapons used include the Ta'as 7.62 Galil, H&K PSG 1 and MP5, the Parker Hale 82 and Finnish Tikka Finlander .223, Mauser SP66 or SR98, and Accuracy International AW-F sniper rifles, Beretta and Remington shotguns, Browning HP 9 mm and SIG-Sauer P228 pistols.

TAG/OAT
The TAG/OAT designation of the SASR followed the Sydney Hilton bomb explosion, which highlighted the need for the regiment to expand and encompass both military and civilian operations. Prime responsibility for counter-terrorist operations lies with the Tactical Assault Group (TAG), with the Offshore Assault Team (OAT) detailed to protect offshore oil installations and shipping. These groups are made up of one of the Sabre squadrons in the third year of its operational cycle. Special emphasis was devoted to internal security during the Sydney 2000 Olympic Games and both units have ample training resources with which to hone their techniques and abilities. These formations have the capability to protect Australian citizens and interests anywhere in the world, though the emphasis is primarily on operations at home.

The Australian SF use a wide range of weapons including the F88 Austeyr, which is the locally manufactured version of the Austrian Steyr-Mannlicher AUG assault rifle which can be seen in this weapons line up, with and without bayonet, with rocket and with grenade launcher (AUG-8) which operates much the same as the US Army's M203. (Steyr Mannlicher AG & Co KG)

Belgium

The **Paratroop Commando Brigade** is Belgium's contribution to ARRC (q.v.), serving in the Multinational Division (Central). It owes its origins to the paratroop and commando units which were formed during the Second World War by the Belgian Government in Exile, the first independent parachute company being established in May 1942. The original complement of 144 soldiers had increased to 210 by January 1943, when the company became a part of the British 6th Airborne Division. A year later it was transferred to the British SAS Brigade for specialised training in clandestine operations. Small parties were later dropped in France and Belgium in areas such as the Ardennes, during July–September 1944, with such tasks as cutting enemy communications, harassing withdrawing enemy units and linking up with the Belgian Secret Army. Belgian commando units were also formed and, from 1940, an independent unit trained in the UK. In that year it fought in Norway, then in 1942 carried out raids in Madagascar, Bruneval, St Nazaire and Dieppe. It became a part of the international No. 10 Commando and fought in the Far East, Sicily, Italy and Greece, as well as in north-west Europe.

They continued after the war, but at the end of the Cold War were reorganised into a single brigade of some 3,000 men, which now consists of: two parachute battalions and one commando battalion, each some 500 in strength and all organised on much the same lines. In support is a parachute armoured reconnaissance battalion (**3rd Lancers**) and parachute artillery (both field and AA batteries), plus engineers, logistics and medical units.

All members of the brigade are volunteers and must attend a five-month commando course, followed by a one-month parachute course which involves seven jumps (including one at night and one from a C-130 with full kit). They must then complete a further four jumps every year to retain their paratroop qualification. They all wear the red beret, but the **1st Battalion** wear in addition the SAS 'dagger' cap badge to signify their wartime links to the British SAS.

Mention must also be made of the Specialised Reconnaissance Teams (ESR) first raised in 1961 and officially disbanded in 1994, who were Belgium's 'warriors in the shadows', giving close protection to embassy staff (e.g. in Kinshasa, Zaire), rescuing Belgian nationals, etc.

The Belgian Navy also has a small section of about thirty **frogmen**, who are organised, trained and equipped along British SBS lines.

Good close-up of the FN 5.56 mm Minimi Light Support Machine-gun – Para Model. It can be fitted with a 200-round disintegrating belt which comes in a sturdy plastic box and clips directly onto the gun. (Fabrique National)

Their all-black underwater gear gives these specially trained Belgian frogmen an unnerving appearance! Note their special SCUBA diving equipment, also the underwater compass and telescopic weapon sight. (Media Ops, HQ ARRC)

Two Belgian paratroops paddle a Klepper canoe, loaded with their gear. They must normally be able to travel for miles with loads of over 150 lb on their backs. (Media Ops, HQ ARRC)

Brazil

The prime formation of Brazil's special forces is the (**1 Batalhão de Foças Especials**) 1st Special Forces Battalion, though in fact other parts of the Brazilian military have their own elite units capable of carrying out anti-terrorist and counter-insurgency operations. Brazil's first airborne troops began training shortly after the Second World War with American assistance, and when sufficient skills had been learned an indigenous parachute school was opened near Rio de Janeiro (now known as the General Penha Brasil Parachute School) and a parachute brigade was formed. From members of this brigade the Brazilian Special Forces were created in 1953, following the hijack of an internal flight over the Amazon. The formation of the counter-terrorist detachment of the 1st Special Forces Battalion came about in 1983. Like almost all special forces there is no civilian recruitment, so all members must volunteer from other military units and undergo a gruelling fourteen-day selection course with an attrition rate of almost 90 per cent, the survivors then going on to a thirteen-week counter-terrorist training course at a secret base just outside Rio de Janeiro. The training is similar to that undergone by the US Delta Force, with marksmanship, combat shooting, parachuting, heliborne insertion and fast-roping all covered, along with a special emphasis on long-range patrols and intelligence gathering in varied environments to cater for Brazil's vast area and varied terrain. The teams in which the CT Detachment operate are larger than average, with up to twenty-four men.

Training and contacts outside Brazil are relatively few, but they have a close association with the US 1st SFOD-D and 7th Special Forces Group that goes back to their inception, and also with the Portuguese GOE. Internally they train and operate with all the federal and state police agencies.

The Brazilian Navy **Combat Diver's Group (GRUMEC)** was formed in 1970 after some officers and enlisted men had been sent to the United States and France, in order to complete the SEAL and *Nageur de Combat* courses. Consisting of fairly large groups of between ten and twenty men, they specialise in discreet infiltration of enemy terrain, sabotage of enemy shipping, harbour installations and oil-rigs and the cutting of enemy supply lines, as well as intelligence gathering. They can insert from almost any kind of vehicle or platform, including ships, fast patrol boats, pneumatic boats, aircraft, helicopters and submarines, and use open-, semi-closed- and closed-circuit diving gear. Training for combat divers lasts over six months and is very gruelling. The GRUMEC course has four phases and takes place at the Brazilian Navy Diving and Submarines Centre (CIAMA), in Niterói City, close to Rio de Janeiro, which also trains conventional divers and submarine crews. The course starts with five weeks' instruction in open-circuit SCUBA diving and the basics of diving. The second phase emphasises physical training and stamina development and lasts another five weeks, culminating in the famous Hell Week, where the candidates are psychologically and bodily tested for more than a hundred hours without respite. In the third phase the candidates learn about amphibious reconnaissance and attack, using closed-circuit diving gear. The fourth phase is devoted to ground operations: raids, terrain orientation, riverine and

This member of the Brazilian Special Forces carries the Colt Firearms M4 Weapons System which is derived from the M16A2 assault rifle and incorporates such modifications as a 4x32 Trijicon Advanced Combat Optical Gunsight and the 40 mm M203 grenade launcher. (Specialforces.net)

jungle environment actions, survival, special warfare action planning, hand to hand fighting, etc. After graduation the combat diver will take part in a thorough training programme and will also take a series of extension courses in several areas such as military climbing, static-line and free-fall parachuting, intelligence gathering and explosives.

Besides special warfare and amphibious operations, GRUMEC is also employed in an anti-kidnapping role, with a group specially trained to retake installations (oil-rigs, ships, etc.), as well as rescuing hostages from criminals and terrorists. This group is called **GRUMEC Retake and Rescue Special Group** (the Portuguese acronym being **GERR/MEC**).

Equipment

Besides the Heckler & Kock K MP5 and Colt 1911 .45, the members of the CT Detachment are proficient in the use of machete and dagger. Shotguns include the Remington M870 and the indigenously produced ENARM Pentagun. The favoured sniping rifle is the Heckler & Koch PSG 1.

GRUMEC weaponry is similar to that used by the US Navy SEALs, including the M16 rifle, pistols, 9 mm submachine -guns, plastic explosives, and magnetic limpet mines.

Canada

Today's Canadian paratroopers can trace their roots through the **Canadian Airborne Regiment** back to two highly distinguished units of the Second World War, namely the **1st Canadian Parachute Battalion** and the **1st Special Service Force**. The 1st Can Para Bn was established on 1 July 1942 and, after training in Fort Benning, Georgia, and later at the newly established Parachute Training Centre in Shilo, Manitoba, left Canada for the UK in July 1943 and joined the British 6th Airborne Division. Subsequently they saw active service on D-Day, then in Belgium and Holland, and took part in the airborne crossing of the Rhine and the subsequent operations into Germany. The unit was disbanded in June 1945, following its return to Canada. The 1st SSF was formed on 10 July 1942 as a joint US–Canadian formation and after training in Montana the Devil's Brigade, as it was later called, deployed first to the Aleutians in the summer of 1943, then to Italy in November 1943, where it saw action in the mountains, then at Anzio, and was the first Allied unit to enter Rome. Subsequently it fought in northern Italy, then in southern France and north-west Europe.

Since the Second World War paratrooping has been preserved in Canada through such units as the **Canadian Special Air Service Company**, the **Mobile Striking Force**, the **Defence of Canada Force** and the **Canadian Airborne Regiment**. Sadly all have now been disbanded – the Airborne Regiment (about 600 men) being the last to go in 1995. However, paratrooping has continued in the Canadian armed forces, with the three small jump companies – one with each of the PPCLI (Princess Patricia's Canadian Light Infantry), 3RCR (Royal Canadian Regiment) and

'Go! Go! Go!' A Canadian paratrooper leaves the aircraft as the jumpmaster gives him the green light. (Canadian Ab Forces Museum)

R22eR (Royal 22e Regiment), at Valcartier, Petawawa and Edmonton respectively. There are some ninety paratroopers in each company.

Chile

Chile's special forces began their history in 1965 when the Parachute and Special Forces School at Peldehue was opened with advice and training from the USA. The **1st Battalion Airborne Forces** was then raised on 2 April 1968, and was operational within two years. It is both a paratroop battalion and a special forces unit, with a stringent selection process eliminating almost 80 per cent of candidates. For the successful there is then still more training at home and in Panama, Fort Benning, USA, Argentina and Brazil, making them some of the best-trained special forces in South America. Operating as a squadron directly under the High Command, they played a major part in the overthrow of the Allende regime by General Pinochet in 1973. They also engaged in the Andes against Communist insurgents.

One parachute battalion is under the control of the Air Force, while the **Boinas Negras Special Forces/Commando Battalion** is an Army formation. There is also a naval unit of combat divers, trained by US SEALs, based at Viña del Mar and Valparaíso and assigned to the Chilean Marines.

In addition to their black berets, Chilean special forces are distinguished by their *corvo*, a curved jungle knife with which they are very proficient.

A party of Chilean Buzos Tacticos de l'Armada (Navy SF commandos) from the combat swimmers battalion, drag their Zodiac inflatable ashore. (Specialforces.net)

China

The first Chinese special forces were US-trained paratroops, disaffected elements of the Kuomintang Army who elected to remain behind on the mainland after the Nationalists' defeat and departure to Taiwan. From this base airborne forces were built up and first saw action in Korea. By the 1960s there were three full airborne divisions to oppose the Nationalist threat, who were in fact used primarily to guard key installations and the Party elite. There are also special reconnaissance infantry divisions and naval combat divers. Little precise information is available on any of these units. Also in more recent times, coinciding with China's attempts at hosting the Olympics, more modern CT units have been established along Western lines.

Denmark

Denmark is yet another small European country which has had considerable influence on a worldwide scale. Their current parachute commandos (LRRP), the **Jaegerkorpset**, can trace their ancestry back to the two-battalion Jaeger Korps which was formed in the late eighteenth century by King Christian VII from skilled woodsmen and other government employees, to serve during time of war as deep amphibious reconnaissance against the enemy. The present unit was established in late 1961 and strongly resembles its Swedish counterpart. Initially specially selected officers were sent to attend the US Ranger School, then went on attachment to the British SAS. In 1964, it established its own training centre at Ålborg in North Jutland, where volunteers from any of the three services who have at least one year's unblemished service receive their initial training. This begins with an eight-week patrol course, which they must pass before going on to further training which includes both frogman and free-fall parachute courses. The former is run by the naval equivalent of the *Jaegerkorpset*, the **Froemandskorpset (Naval Frogman's Corps)**. As with all SF troops, other specialist training includes courses in demolitions, first aid, communications and weapons.

Having successfully completed this arduous course, they are put on probation for a year, with only the very best eventually selected to join the elite small band of parachute commandos, which is currently just company-sized. It is also of interest that all Danish Army officer cadets must attend courses in both *Jaegerkorpset* patrolling and airborne operations before being commissioned.

As the Danes have no large helicopters the *Jaegerkorpset* often gets helicopter support from the British and Germans.

The *Froemandskorpset* was formed in 1957 as part of the naval diving school, after a small number of officers were sent to the USA to train with SEALs. Then in 1970, it became a separate organisation whose tasks include beach reconnaissance, underwater demolitions and similar frogman tasks, but also, the boarding of suspect vessels and harbour protection. The unit saw active service during the Gulf War and is now stationed at the Kongsore Naval Station.

Two Danish paratroop commandos in a Klepper boat having shipped their paddles and taken aim with their weapons. (Specialforces.net)

Egypt

The Egyptian Army has placed considerable importance on airborne and commando forces since its inception. At present there are two airborne brigades, one parachute brigade and seven special forces/commando groups in the Egyptian Order of Battle (ORBAT). Although fewer in numbers than their Syrian counterpart, the Egyptian special forces nevertheless exceed some 15,000 men and about a hundred helicopters. They are manned by high-quality manpower and led by the best officers.

The first Egyptian parachute-trained unit was formed in 1959, shortly after the Sinai Campaign, becoming operational in September 1961. In 1963, a newly formed battalion of paratroopers and commandos landed at Sanacu airport, Yemen, seizing major vantage points within the city and its environs and fighting against the Imam's royalists. By 1967 the Egyptian airborne and commando force had grown to several thousand men and in 1969 they were combined as special forces and used frequently in the Suez Canal Campaign. Now called **A-Saiqa (Lightning) Commandos**, in one particularly successful raid they crossed the Canal during the night of 9 July 1969 and attacked an Israeli tank encampment near Port Tawfiq, destroying several tanks. During the 1973 October War, the Egyptian commandos spearheaded the Canal crossing operations, with two parachute brigades, two airborne assault brigades and seven commando groups taking part. Trained special forces acted as spearhead on 6

October, scaling the Israeli sand ramparts along the Suez Canal and setting up anti-tank ambushes fighting off the IDF reinforcements. A special unit of naval commandos also neutralised Israeli underwater oil pipes. Meanwhile, further south, the **130th Marine Brigade** crossed the Great Bitter Lakes and used naval/paratroop frogmen to raid Israeli positions on the eastern shores. Heliported commando teams were also flown into Sinai behind Israeli lines to rupture IDF communication centres and delay incoming reinforcements, one group blocking an entire reserve armoured division for several hours near Romani in northern Sinai. The largest force, of battalion size, made for Ras Sudar, south of Suez, where it was badly mauled by Israeli Air Force F-4 Phantoms and IDF paratroops. The Egyptian **182nd Paratroop Brigade**, operating on the West Bank, fought a savage battle with Israeli paras advancing towards Ismailiya during the final stages of the war. Egyptian naval commandos also operated before the war. During two nights, on 15 November 1969 and 5 February 1970, frogmen attacked and sank two Israeli merchant ships and one naval transport in two daring attacks.

Since the peace with Israel, the Egyptian special forces have not been idle. Its counter-terrorist unit, **Force 777**, has been used in several operations. One of the first was at Nicosia airport, Cyprus, where Palestinian guerrillas had hijacked a Cyprus Airways jet flying in from Cairo. Egyptian commandos landed in Cyprus, but due to mistaken identity clashed

Egyptian paratroopers boarding a Boeing CH-47 Chinook helicopter. Remarkably the first Model 114/CH-47 Chinook flew in September 1961. Constantly modified, the current version, the MH-47E, is ideal for carrying out five-hour, deep-penetration, clandestine missions over a 300-nautical mile radius. (Patrick Allen)

disastrously with the Cypriot police. In another incident, Palestinian Abu Nidal terrorists hijacked Egyptair Flight 648 at Athens Airport and flew to Malta, having shot five Egyptian hostages. Force 777 was flown by C-130 to Malta, but attacked without sufficient intelligence, virtually blindly. No fewer than eighty men were present, but when the assault force moved in the attack once again ended in disaster. After a six-hour gun battle, having lost the element of surprise, fifty-seven passengers were killed. Following these fiascos, Force 777 was totally reorganised and retrained and mainly used since in the anti-fundamentalist campaign inside Egypt.

Equipment
Standard fatigues are green on tan or sand-coloured camouflage combat dress. Paratroops wear cloth-covered jump helmets. The former standard Soviet camouflage pattern was replaced with new webbing gear. The A-Saiqa commandos normally wear standard desert-colour sand-brown camouflage uniforms with black boots. The commando black beret is worn with the national eagle badge over the left eye.
   The A-Saiqa commando normally has a 9 mm Beretta M1951 S automatic, AKM 7.62 mm assault rifle and Dragunov SVD sniper rifle.

Finland

In 1996, the Finnish Defence Forces began a new kind of readiness training aimed at forming a wartime unit capable of carrying out international crisis-management duties. They pride themselves on being one of the few countries in the world to give conscripts professional-level special-forces training. Conscripts willing to be trained for service with SF have to apply for a position, then are tested for their psychological and physical suitability for the specialised training. Both paratroopers and marine commandos, then serve 362 days in the military, but not rangers. Ranger troops need longer detailed reconnaissance training in addition to the more traditional survival and ranger activities.

France

In 1992, France followed the example set by the USA and the UK by combining its special forces under one joint operational command, the **Commandement des opérations spéciales (COS)**. Before this happened, the SF of the French Navy, Army and Air Forces that form the **FAR (Forces d'action rapide)**, the French equivalent of the UK Rapid Reaction Forces, and the French intelligence service units, the DGSE (*Direction générale de la sécurité* exterieure), were all available to be used, but lacked a joint command structure. This has now been achieved, the mission of the new HQ being 'to plan, co-ordinate and conduct at the command level all operations carried out by units that are specifically organised, trained and equipped to attain military or paramilitary objectives as defined by the Armed Forces Chief of Staff'. To achieve this mission the command has under its permanent control certain elite units, known as *le premier cercle* comprising:

• **1 Régiment parachutiste d'infanterie de marine (1 RPIMa)** – ex-colonial troops with no connection to naval infantry units in spite of the reference to that branch, and the **Détachement aérien des opérations spéciales (DAOS)** – the Special Operations Aviation Unit, both of whom come under the **Groupement spécial autonome (GSA)** – Special Independent Command. 1 RPIMa is very similar to the SAS; indeed they could be said to have their roots in the French SAS units of the Second World War. Their main missions are intelligence (LRRP), special operations and anti-terrorism (with GIGN).
• five naval assault commando units – **Jaubert**, **de Montfort**, **de Penfentenyo**, **Trepel** and **Hubert** – with the **Groupe de combat en milieu clos (GCMC)**, the Close Quarters Combat Team which is part of the **Commandement des fusiliers-marins commandos (COFUSCO)** – Naval Infantry

and SF Command. All five commando units are similar to the UK SBS and the US SEALs, with whom they maintain strong links, but Hubert is even more special than the rest as it is composed entirely of underwater swimmers (*nageurs de combat*).
• **Commando parachutiste de l'air no 10 (CPA 10)** – an Air Force commando unit which, for example, launched operations to rescue the crew of a downed Mirage in Bosnia. Some are HALO and HAHO qualified
• **Escadrille des hélicoptères spéciaux (EHS)** – a special operations helicopter squadron
• **Division des opérations spéciales (DOS)** – Special Operations Division (Aviation)

As well as these elite units others, such as the police's GIGN (*Groupe d'intervention de la Gendarmerie Nationale*) or other specialised French armed forces units may participate in anti-terrorist missions.
   These elite SF are trained to carry out missions in four main areas:

• military assistance – to include training and advising foreign military personnel, especially in areas of Africa where many countries have defence treaties with France; operations can include humanitarian actions by military personnel
• military operations support – using their specialised skills such as long-range recce, day and night assault, search and rescue (e.g. of downed pilots), unit liaison and peacekeeping
• counter-terrorism – including resolving hostage incidents and the evacuation of French nationals from a foreign territory
• 'influence' operations – what the British call 'hearts and minds' operations, including participating in civil affairs and PSYOPS

Men of 3 RPIMa on board a helicopter. They are part of the French Rapid Intervention Force. (Patrick Allen)

1 RIPMa

With a history stretching back to 1 August 1940, when General de Gaulle gave orders to form the *1 compaigne d'infanterie de l'air*, this Bayonne-based unit has always lived up to its motto, *'Qui ose gagne'* (Who dares wins). It saw its first action in March 1941, when five French parachutists were dropped in the Morbihan region of France to sabotage a *Luftwaffe* unit. After the war, they were used in Indo-China then Algeria (now brigade-sized). In 1958 the brigade became the training brigade for colonial airborne troops. Then in 1960, the Overseas Airborne Brigade became known as the **Naval Airborne Infantry Brigade**. Two years later, the unit was disbanded and 1 RIPMa came into being. Since then they have seen action in various parts of the world, in particular in Africa, including Zaire, Chad, Rwanda and Congo-Brazzaville.

As with all SF units, volunteers for 1 RIPMa must undergo a searching introductory period, the successful candidates going on to a nine-month induction course of commando training, on which the attrition rate is over 50 per cent. This *rapière* course is a requirement for all ranks, so that the physical stamina of all new members can be evaluated.

The operational nucleus of the regiment is the **RAPAS squad** (*recherche et action spécialiste* – intelligence and special operations). Each is made up of ten commandos, led by an experienced officer or NCO. It is divided into a four-man command cell (team leader, radio operator, communications specialist and medic) and three two-man teams. The team leader normally has experience of the area in which they will be operating. RAPAS teams are completely self-contained, independent and equipped with both long-range communications equipment and a wide variety

RAPAS Training and Equipment
RAPAS squads regularly train in the jungles of French Guiana and the deserts of Djibouti, and they have built a special urban training facility at Pau in the Pyrenees. They use a wide range of weapons, many of which have been specially adapted for their needs. Personal weapons include pistols such as the 5.56 mm Pamas and the Smith & Wesson, the 9 mm Mini-Uzi with silencer, the H&K MP5 and various assault rifles. Heavier weapons include 81 mm and 120 mm mortars, MILAN anti-tank weapons, and Stinger and Mistral air defence systems.

of weapons, so that they can deal with a substantial enemy threat. Each two-man team specialises in a particular skill, such as sabotage, shooting, climbing, breaking and entering, etc. They can be grouped together into larger detachments (say of 150–160 men) for a particular operation.

The basic organisation of 1 RIPMa is: RHQ, command and general services company, training company and three RAPAS companies – the training company can form a fourth RAPAS company if needed. The companies specialise in certain areas:

- 1 Company – non-urban operations, water crossings and VIP escorts
- 2 Company – urban warfare, explosives, sabotage, breaking and entering, and sniping
- 3 Company – fire support with heavy mortars, air defence and reconnaissance in light all-terrain vehicles

Naval Assault Commando Units
Most frequently deployed of all the personnel in the French armed forces, three of the five commando units are based at Lorient and a further one each at Toulon and Djibouti. Stand-by equipment is stored for

them at all three bases, the equipment at Toulon being able to be loaded onto an aircraft carrier or a TCM at short notice. Each element takes its turn at being on immediate call, so they can be at as little as six hours' notice to move. This gives them tremendous flexibility and means that they are available for widespread and varied operations at a moment's notice.

Each commando unit comprises four twenty-man platoons, usually divided into two combat teams. Each team has a twenty-man HQ section ECT (*Element de commandement et de transmissions*), an assault team, a reconnaissance team and a fire support team. The HQ contains in addition to the commander and his 2IC, a naval intelligence officer, two communications specialists, two radio operators, three pilots and some ten more men. The assault team's main mission is to take and hold a beach-head, and they are backed up by the support platoon with heavy fire support. The recce platoon's task is to reconnoitre beaches with the aim of deciding which can be held, with the platoon's personnel responsible for holding the area until relieved. Follow-up elements can come in by helicopter, either abseiling or parachuting into the sea or by submarine or surface ship. The former is normally effected from a Puma or Super-Frelon helicopter some twelve miles from the objective, so that it is virtually undetectable. Half a platoon can be offloaded from a Puma in less than a minute, complete with a Zodiac inflatable. A Super-Frelon can take twelve men and two Zodiacs.

There are just sixteen men in the *Groupe de combat en milieu clos* (GCMC), divided into two teams of eight men, although if necessary they can be supplemented by other personnel trained in maritime counter-terrorism – for example, they work

regularly with Commando Hubert. GCMC has the special mission of boarding a ship which is in terrorist hands, using Hurricane or Zodiac rigid-hull craft. Each member of the seventeen-man team has his own speciality, such as weapons, munitions, demolitions, medical, diving, surface-water operations, etc.

Commando Hubert is an underwater action unit based at Toulon quite near the military diving school. Volunteers for this elite unit must have at least four years' service in the French Navy and be qualified divers. In addition to successfully completing the Combat Swimmers' Course they must also become master parachutists. Those who pass will join their unit for three years, normally extended to six. Commando Hubert is divided into two companies: the 1st is the operational unit, the 2nd combat support. Attached is the naval vessel *Poseidon*, which serves as a floating base for the combat swimmers and their two-man swimmer delivery vehicles (PSM – *propulseur sous-marin*). 1 Company has fifty combat swimmers divided into four platoons: A is command and control, and is equipped with Hurricane rigid craft; B is counter-terrorism; C is underwater operations; and D is reconnaissance and support operations. Personnel can be selected from each platoon to make up a suitable force for a particular operation.

Some French air commandos from **CPA 10** *who work closely with the Special Helicopter Operations (DOS/H) are seen here waiting to board their helicopters* (Patrick Allen)

Commando parachutiste de l'air no 10

CPA 10, together with the *Division des opérations spéciales hélicoptères* (DOS/H), came under the control of COS in 1994. Volunteers must be twenty-seven or twenty-eight years old, sergeant and above, qualified commandos (at level 2) and with at least five years' service. Successful applicants are then given specialised training in selected fields such as combat parachutist, sniper, search and rescue specialist, etc. The unit is company-sized (125 all ranks), divided into an HQ, three combat detachments and a training and logistics element. One of the three combat detachments has HALO/HAHO capability. Their missions include laser target designation, securing and marking LZs (Landing Zones) for future airborne operations, reconnaissance and the restoration of airfield facilities. They were used both during the Gulf War and in Bosnia for laser target designation.

Escadrille des hélicoptères spéciaux (EHS)

Based at Cazaux, the unit's mission is to maintain five pilots and five crew mechanics to carry out all COS missions. When they are

A légionnaire from the CEA (Support & Recce Company) of 2 REI, pictured during operations in Chad. *(MPL International Ltd)*

A légionnaire combat diver from the DINOPS team of 6 RE during a recce up river in his Klepper canoe at dusk. He is armed with a silenced 9 mm Uzi SMG. *(MPL International Ltd)*

undertaking combat search and rescue operations, they use a pair of Puma helicopters and are supported by such elements of the French Air Forces as fighter-bomber cover and AWACS (for surveillance and navigation). The highly experienced pilots all have at least 1,500 flying hours on helicopters, including 300–400 hours' night flying, day and night landings on naval vessels, etc. In fact they are some of the most experienced helicopter pilots in the world.

Division des opérations spéciales (DOS)
Attached to the Air Crew Training Centre at Toulouse is a group of seventeen Transail aircraft crews. Other C-130 Hercules crews are available as necessary in Orléans. Each DOS crew consists of two pilots, a navigator and weapons systems officer, a flight mechanic and a ground mechanic. All are highly experienced and only require some three hours preparation before setting out on a mission, which might be in support of CPA 10, 1 RIPMa or Naval Commandos. Only DOS has the capability of undertaking helicopter refuelling operations.

Légion étrangère
Although not a part of France's special forces, the elite **Légion étrangère** (Foreign Legion) has long been used for special operations all over the world on behalf of France. It was formed in the nineteenth century (1831) to help control the French colonies in Africa. Until 1962 its headquarters was at Sidi Bel Abbes in Algeria, but after Algerian independence it moved to Corsica, with a reception HQ at Aubagne, near Marseille. It has always been composed of foreign mercenaries, commanded by French officers, although nowadays there are about one-third Frenchmen in its ranks. The Foreign Legion fought bravely in both World Wars and afterwards in Indo-China. Its epic defence as the main element of the garrison of Dien Bien Phu (March–May 1954) ended in surrender to a much larger force. Later in 1961, in Algeria, one Foreign Legion regiment mutinied in support of the settlers in order to try to prevent Algerian independence. Despite its outstanding combat record it was disbanded in disgrace. More recently, in 1988, when the French Army was drastically reduced in size, the Foreign Legion was cut to 7,500 and withdrew from some of its overseas bases, but still remains an important element of the French Army.

The Legion is responsible for its own recruiting and training, which is undertaken by two of its regiments – **1er Régiment étranger** (1 RE) at Aubagne, where all new recruits begin their service and **4er Régiment étranger** (4 RE) at Casteinaudar which is responsible for both recruit and NCO training. Aubagne is now the spiritual 'home' of the Legion where its museum and band are located. Combat units are as follows:

1er Régiment étranger de cavalerie (1 REC). Stationed at Orange, it is part of the French 6th Light Armoured Division. It comprises three armoured car companies and an APC-borne infantry company.

2ème Régiment étranger d'infanterie (2 REI). Stationed at Nimes, it has served in nearly every colonial campaign through the years.

3ème Régiment étranger d'infanterie (3 REI). Stationed at Kourou, French Guiana. The Legion's jungle warfare specialists, it also has responsibility for the security of the French missile launching site there.

Légionnaire *sentry from 3ème* Régiment étranger d'infanterie *(3 REI), wearing a kepi and armed with a 5.56 mm FAMAS rifle, stands guard outside the main gate to Quartier Forget, HQ 3 REI, in French Guiana. (MPL International Ltd)*

5ème Régiment étranger (5 RE). Stationed on French islands in the Pacific, it is responsible for Mururoa Atoll (French nuclear weapons test site).

6ème Régiment étranger de génie (6 REG). Raised in 1984, it is based at Plain d'Albion, and maintains engineer detachments abroad, including **Détachement d'intervention opérationnelle subaquatique** (combat swimmers and underwater EOD).

2ème Régiment étranger de parachutistes (2 REP). This rapid deployment airborne/commando regiment is stationed in Corsica at Calvi. It comprises six companies, all specially trained in different forms of combat, although there is regular cross-training between companies.

13ème Demi-brigade légion étranger (13 DBLE). This half brigade is stationed at Djibouti and contains an armoured car squadron, an infantry company and a support company (with mortars and MILAN anti-tank missiles).

Détachement de légion étranger à Mayotte (DLEM). This special detachment is responsible for the island of Mayotte in the Indian Ocean.

Selection and Training
Volunteers come from all over the world (over 100 different countries) except, in theory, France.

Légionnaire *from* 2ème Régiment étranger de parachutistes *(2 REP), armed with a 5.56 mm FAMAS rifle, on patrol in Senegal.* (MPL International Ltd)

A légionnaire *paratrooper from* 2ème Régiment étranger de parachutistes *(2 REP) aims his 5.56 mm FN Minimi machine-gun whilst on exercise in the Corsican mountains. The Minimi can use either 5.56 mm belt ammunition or standard NATO 30 round magazines, as shown here, making it a very flexible section automatic weapon.* (MPL International Ltd)

However, the Legion now contains about one-third Frenchmen who have got around the ban by pretending to be Swiss, French Canadian or Belgian. On enlistment they are given an alias, then attend a punishing three-week induction training period during which they can leave of their own volition or be compulsorily discharged, but if they stick it out they are bound to serve for a further five months. The first year consists of training with 4 RE, much of which is conducted on Corsica. Great emphasis is put on physical training and marksmanship. After basic training some will be selected for specialist training (e.g. as a signaller or an engineer), whilst potential NCOs must attend a physically demanding eight-week course prior to promotion to corporal, then a fourteen-week course before promotion to sergeant.

Légion étrangère Uniform

Whilst the *légionnaires* wear standard French uniform, they do have certain distinctive items of dress, e.g. *le kepi blanc* (this is actually a standard blue kepi but with a white cover). For normal daily wear all (including the paratroopers of 2 REP) wear a green beret. Officers are permitted to wear a special green waistcoat under their service dress top.

Paratroops

The 11th Parachute Division, which is some 11,000 strong, is stationed at Tarbes in the Midi-Pyrenees region of southern France, although a fair proportion of the division is always overseas on operations or training. They are long-service professionals, who continue the long tradition of paratroop operations since the Second World War (e.g. Indo-China, Suez, Zaire), making them one of the most widely experienced paratroop forces of any nation. They are currently part of the French rapid intervention force, which also contains the 4th Airmobile Division, 6th Light Armoured Division, 27th Alpine Division and the 9th Marine Light Infantry Division. The division is divided into two brigades, containing a total of seven battalion-sized paratroop units, one of which is 1 RPIMa and another is 2 REP from the *Légion étrangère*. The remaining five are: 1 and 9 RCP (both light infantry), 3, 6 and 8 RPIMa.

Paratroop Uniforms

Distinctive items are: red berets, worn by all paras, except for 2 REP who wear *Légion* green; paratroop wings in silver on the right breast. Apart from these two items they wear standard French Army uniforms.

A special forces frogman from Commando Hubert swims up river with only his mask and moderated Mini-Uzi submachine-gun above the surface of the water. (MPL International Ltd)

Germany

Just as with other NATO nations, Germany has troops in the Allied Rapid Reaction Corps (ARRC), in the form of a complete armoured division. They also have specialised elite troops of divisional/brigade size: a mountain infantry division (**Gebirgsjaeger**); a parachute infantry brigade (**Fallschirmjaeger**) and a commando brigade (**Kommando Spezialkrafte**).

Gebirgsjaeger

Germany, like Italy and France, has always had a small number of units trained in mountain and winter warfare; for example, prior to the First World War, there were ski battalions in the Alpine Corps. However, after experiencing the winter conditions on the Vosges Front during 1914–15 it was decided to form specially trained and equipped units to operate in snowy, mountainous areas. They wore a grey-green uniform with green facings and a mountaineering cap with the edelweiss (a small, white Alpine flower) badge on the side. One *Gebirgsjaeger* officer, was the legendary 'Desert Fox', Field Marshal Erwin Rommel. Between the wars the mountain troop tradition was maintained in some of the Bavarian units of the German Army, and these were gradually increased in size with the rise to power of the Nazi Party, followed by the *Anschluss* of Austria in 1938, after which the three mountain divisions of the Austrian Army were absorbed. By 1940, a fourth division had been formed and this expansion continued, there being at least seven complete mountain divisions and a number of other units, formed by the end of 1941, plus one *Skijaeger* division. Mountain troops fought on all fronts, being particularly effective where their special skills could be put to good use. In general they were more lightly equipped than normal infantry divisions and had few vehicles, most of their transportation being horses, both to draw the wagons and to act as pack animals. Mountain troops claimed the honour of advancing farther into Russia than any other German soldier, when they raised their flag on Mount Elbrus in the Caucasus.

This long history and tradition, and the skills, have been maintained by **1 Gebirgsdivision**, which is stationed in the Munich area of Germany (*Wehrbereichskommando VI (WBK VI)* – Military District VI).

As can be seen from the diagram (opposite), the main infantry element is **Gebirgsjaegerbrigade 23**, but the division also has considerable armour, artillery and engineering. There is a complete armoured brigade (**Panzerbrigade 36**) equipped with Leopard 2 main battle tanks, a complete engineer brigade (**Pionierlehrbrigade 60**), plus supporting artillery (**Artillerieregiment 4**) containing both guns and missiles, an AA regiment (**Gebirgspanzerflugabwehrkanonenregiment 8**) equipped with forty-two AA tanks, a reconnaissance battalion (**Gebirgspanzeraufklarungsbataillon 8**),

This KSK trooper looks more like something out of Star Wars as he aims his weapon in full anti-terrorist gear. (KSK Personalwebetrupp)

and all the other normal supporting arms and services, but modified to suit the division's special needs. Despite all this sophistication, however, as the accompanying photographs show, the mountain soldiers have lost none of their basic skills and train under the most adverse weather and terrain conditions.

Fallschirmjaeger

The Versailles Treaty restricted the building of powered aircraft in Germany and thus forced potential aviators to take up gliding, inadvertently providing the Germans with a ready source of glider-trained pilots! From the 1920s, more and more skilled pilots were trained and soon began to win all the prizes in international gliding contests. At the same time came the start of parachuting, not just as a means for pilots to escape from damaged aircraft, but also for inserting lightly equipped forces behind enemy lines. Germany

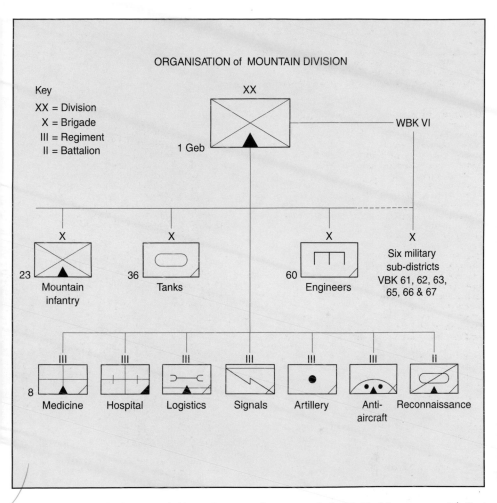

ORGANISATION of MOUNTAIN DIVISION

Key
XX = Division
X = Brigade
III = Regiment
II = Battalion

XX
1 Geb

WBK VI

X
23 — Mountain infantry

X
36 — Tanks

X
60 — Engineers

X
Six military sub-districts VBK 61, 62, 63, 65, 66 & 67

III
8 — Medicine

III
Hospital

III
Logistics

III
Signals

III
Artillery

III
Anti-aircraft

II
Reconnaissance

took the lead in the development of airborne forces under the guidance of Major-General Karl Student, 'father' of the *Fallschirmjaeger*, who was given the task in 1938 of forming the first airborne division as part of the *Luftwaffe*. Although ready for operations at the beginning of the war, the paratroopers were not used during the invasion of Poland, but showed their abilities (and their frailties) spearheading the daring assaults on Norway and Denmark. Hitler was quick to appreciate the potential of airborne forces, giving them important roles in the attack on the West in May 1940, when they were used to capture the seemingly impregnable Belgian fortress of Eben-Emael and key bridges along the Maas. The first time they were used *en masse* was for the invasion of Crete in May 1941, where they managed to capture the island but suffered horrendous casualties, convincing Hitler that they should not be employed in what way again. Indeed, the victory in Crete became the 'graveyard of

German parachuting', but had the very opposite effect upon the British and Americans, who began building up their own airborne forces as quickly as they could.

Student was himself mortified by the slaughter from which German parachuting never recovered and this was virtually the last time that German *Fallschirmjaeger* were dropped into action in such large numbers, the ten parachute divisions thereafter being used as normal infantry. They were tough, well-trained troops and showed their fighting abilities in such places as the defence of Monte Cassino in Italy in May 1943 and on the Russian front. They were also used for such daring raids as the rescue of Benito Mussolini, when he was 'snatched', from under the very noses of the Allies by a small number of airborne soldiers, led by Otto Skorzeny, who was awarded the Knight's Cross for this exploit. They were also used during the initial part of the German offensive in the Ardennes in late 1944, but this was an absolute shambles and few of the 800-plus paratroopers who took part, actually landed in the correct locations. Nevertheless, the haphazard nature of the drop added to the general Allied paranoia basically caused by small numbers of German soldiers wearing Allied uniforms and equipped with Allied vehicles, who got behind Allied lines and tried to sabotage communications of all types and to cause chaos generally – even the Supreme Commander, General Dwight D. Eisenhower, was confined to his headquarters because it was thought that these infiltrators were being sent to assassinate him!

After the war, the German airborne brigade was reformed in 1956 and rapidly grew to divisional size, the main task of the three brigades (**Luftbrigade 25, 26 and 27**) being purely defensive in the event of a Soviet invasion, namely slowing down the advancing hordes rather than being dropped behind enemy lines. Now they form **Luftlandebrigade 31** and are located in the Oldenburg area.

Kommando Spezialkrafte

Located at Calw in Baden-Württemberg, this brigade-sized commando unit, known as the KSK, was initially formed from men of the commando and deep re-connaissance companies, which were integral component parts of the three West German airborne brigades (25, 26 and 27) of the Cold War era. Since the

Kommando Spezialkräfte
Leiter der Personalwerbung

formation of the KSK in the mid-1990s, the unit has been growing in strength and is now reaching its full strength. It comprises an HQ (the commander is a brigadier), four commando companies, a long-range reconnaissance company, an HQ and communications company and a logistics company (which includes maintenance of parachutes as well as normal administrative requirements such as transport, vehicle maintenance, medical, etc.), together with its own training centre. Each company has four platoons, one of which contains operatives who are highly trained in hostage rescue. In addition, platoons also specialise in different methods of operating: ground infiltration, airborne operations, amphibious operations and mountainous or Arctic conditions. Unlike the police GSG9 the KSK is not constrained by having to operate only within German frontiers. It is thus, in an emergency, able to protect or to rescue German nationals at risk in overseas areas of conflict, as well as dealing with more localised terrorist situations. Like so many other SF units the basic sub-unit is the four-man patrol and the long-range reconnaissance company consists of forty four-man teams, each capable of operating on their own to obtain information. They maintain constant contact with their HQ by long-range communication links (via satellite and/or HF radio).

Training, like that of all other commando units is exacting, as everyone must reach then maintain a peak of physical fitness and mental agility. They must also be able to take part in air deployment, either by helicopter (using the Model G version of the CH-53 Stallion Sikorsky heavy transport helicopter which is locally manufactured in Germany by VFM-Fokker) or by parachute (they must train using both HALO and HAHO techniques).

No matter the weather training must continue. Gebirgsjaeger *firing their MG3 GPMGs. Although the basic design dates back over 50 years, the MG3 is one of the best GPMGs in the world.* (Presse und Oefflichtsarbeit Bundeswehr)

A German SF trooper with the IKAR snappling device after roping down. (Col D Eshel)

Excellent shot of Gebirgsjaeger engaging the enemy after skiing into a fire position. They are armed with the H&K G3 battle rifle, which is in service with more than 50 countries. (Presse und Oefflichtsarbeit Bundeswehr)

Greece

The Greek special forces are some of the most modern in the world, with units capable of operating on land, sea and in the air. They also have the longest recorded history of raiding operations of any country in the world – going back to such Homeric tales as that of the Trojan Horse operation!

In more modern times, namely during the Second World War, the Hellenic special forces organisation originated in the Middle East when, following the Battle of Crete in May 1941, the Hellenic Government was established in Egypt and began to create new units for the Hellenic Army. One of these was the 'Company of the Chosen Immortals' established in August 1942, under the command of Major Stephanakis, which had an initial strength of 200 all ranks. Later the unit was renamed: 'The Sacred Company' – the fifth unit to be called by that name in Greek history – and it continued to operate initially in close co-operation with the British SAS, first in North Africa (also attached to the New Zealand Corps and then integrated into the Free French); then later they operated in Italy and in the Dodecanese. They were disbanded at the end of the war.

Reformed during the Greek civil war (1945–50), the nucleus of the ex-Sacred Company was preserved as a raiding force, which combined all the characteristics of the British SAS and SBS, in other words, they were ready for land, sea or air operations. Also in the summer of 1946, the first Mountainous Raiding Warfare Company was formed, to help deal with the problems caused by armed communist groups active in the countryside. Eventually there were forty such companies formed, their mission being to control the spread of communist revolt and conduct operations in the mountainous mainland of Greece. They were active right up until the communist revolt came to an end in 1950.

SPECIAL FORCES OF THE HELLENIC ARMY BADGE
Created by the cadres of the Sacred Company during the Second World War.

Description: A sword surrounded with wings. The sword symbolises the light and noiseless weapons carried by the raiding personnel, while the wings symbolise the effectiveness of airlift operations and accompllishment of missions.

MOTTO: **'Those who dare win'** – Daring is the most essential factor of victory.

In recent times, several reorganisation phases have been necessary. In 1955, with the help of the Americans, the Parachute School was established at Aspropyrgros of Attica, near Athens and the SF Directorate in the Hellenic Army General Staff, with tactical command in Thessaloniki. During 1964–74, SF units participated in operations during the Turkish invasion of Cyprus and sustained thirty-three killed. Recent reorganisation has led to an even more operationally effective, all-volunteer force.

Present organisation
The present Greek SF consist of:

The Special Forces Directorate
1 Parachute Regiment
1 Marine Brigade
1 Special Operations Command
1 Ranger Regiment

Training Centres
Greek SF have three training centres:

Special Forces Training Centre
Unconventional Training Centre
Parachute Training Centre

Men of the Greek Marine Brigade manning a light rigid raider vessel as they speed over the waves. (Greek Special Forces Directorate)

All-round defence. A four-man patrol of Greek SF can produce considerable firepower from their M16 assault rifles and (facing camera) a Colt Firearms M4 Weapons System. (Greek Special Forces Directorate)

MARINE CORPS BADGE

Description: *Argo* the mythological warship of Jason. It is a symbol of amphibious operations, since it was the first ship in history used for the Argonaut Expedition.

MOTTO: **'You must have courage – tomorrow everything will be better'** – Advice that the goddess Athena imparted via Ulysses to the Greek fighters at Troy, when they were thinking to abandon their effort and return home.

Well camouflaged in his snowsuit, a Greek SF trooper waits in ambush. (Greek Special Forces Directorate)

Special forces must be capable of operating in any terrain or climate. Here a Greek Ranger patrol makes its way through mixed woodland. (Greek Special Forces Directorate)

A Greek SF patrol use their ski poles to provide a stable platform as they engage targets. (Greek Special Forces Directorate)

tough group of Greek
marines come ashore.
(Greek Special Forces
Directorate)

Iran

The Iranian armed forces are currently undergoing substantial reorganisation and up-to-date information on its special forces is incomplete.

The Army is organised into a three-tiered force consisting of the regular army, the *Pasdaran* (Islamic Revolutionary Guards Corp–IRGC) and the *Bassidjis* (irregular forces). It is not clear whether the Special Forces Division comes under the command of the regular army, or has become part of the *Pasdaran*. The latter, even if it does not directly control it, could well influence its operational profile, owing to the fact that important strategic and undercover operations could well come under its mission profile.

Under the Shah's regime, the imperial armed forces operated the **25th Airborne Brigade**, trained by the US special forces. A parachute school was also raised and considerable activity included no fewer than fourteen parachute trade insignia, from basic para to senior jumpmaster, indicating that substantial airborne operations were included in training. However, during the Iran–Iraq War the revolutionary forces invested very little in raising a separate special forces unit, and the 25th Airborne was apparently disbanded, possibly following purges. Only small unit assault and patrol functions operated during the war, but the Iranian Army never developed effective long-range penetration and special forces groups.

Reports on Iranian special forces instructors operating in Lebanon (training Hizbullah), Sudan and Bosnia have been verified. Most of these activities include training in sabotage, undercover and guerrilla warfare. Indications also hint that Iranian *Pasdaran* instructors are serving in the Sudanese Army.

Iraq

There are presently ten special forces/commando brigades in the Iraqi establishment, all under the command of the Republican Guards. These formations are regarded as elite infantry units. Apart from these a special forces command operating within the Republican Guard is responsible for internal security. This force included ten special infantry battalions. Precise information about these forces is somewhat lacking since Operation *Desert Storm*. It is assumed that the present SF are incorporated into the Republican Guard formations.

The origins of the Iraqi SF began in 1942, when a parachute company was formed by Royal Air Force levies cadred by British officers and NCOs from the 156th British Parachute Battalion at Habbaniyah airfield. The Iraqi company took part in an action near Corfu in August 1943.

In 1948 a force of some 200 para/commandos fought in Palestine. In 1964 a US 3rd Special Forces team trained and assisted in forming the first **Special Forces Brigade**. By 1973 a second brigade was formed and trained in airmobile warfare. The two brigades fought Kurdish rebels in northern Iraq. During the 1973 October War, the 1st SF Brigade fought several commando actions against IDF armoured forces in night lagers. One was particularly effective during the night of 16/17 October near Tel el-Mal on the Golan. During the Iraq–Iran War, at least four Iraqi special forces brigades were identified by 1985: the **65th, 3rd, 68th and 66th Special Forces Brigades** (the 3rd SF Brigade fought under the Presidential Guard elite).

Before the invasion of Kuwait in August 1990 the Iraqi special forces numbered three brigades, as well as some separate parachute units.

> **Uniform**
> Special forces camouflage utilities, with the Special Forces Brigade insignia: parachute wings, gold or silver wire and red cloth pad underline. Para instructors wear gold wings with black cloth padding underline.

Republic of Ireland

Despite the small size of the Irish Defence Forces (18,000 permanent plus 22,000 reserve), the need for special forces has long been appreciated and the *Sciathan Fianoglach an Airm* – the Army Rangers Wing – was formed in 1980, after a select small number of men from all the Irish armed forces had attended training in the USA. They are now in contact with a wide range of special forces and similar police organisations worldwide, to improve their skills in hostage and other counter-terrorist operations. They cover these missions as well as the more obvious military ones such as raids, ambushes, sabotage, etc., as do all other special forces. It is unlikely that they presently have links to the SAS, but perhaps the improving situation in Northern Ireland will bring this in the future. As with most SF, they use a wide range of weapons which are to be found in their own army and others worldwide. These include the Steyr AUG assault rifle which is made in Austria.

Men of the Irish Rangers Wing (IRW) fire their Steyr AUG assault rifles on the range. (Steyr Mannlicher AG & Co KG)

Israel

The roots of Israel's elite forces can be traced back to the 1930s, when under the leadership of Captain (later Major-General) Charles Orde Wingate, **Special Night Squads** were formed to fight a mobile anti-guerrilla war against Arab marauders. During the Second World War Palestinian Jews fought as volunteers in the British 51st Middle East Commando in Eritrea, as well as in the Special Interrogation Group in North Africa. *Palmach* (*Hagana*) guides also led the British/Australian invasion into Vichy-occupied Syria and Lebanon in June 1941.

After their defeat in the 1948–9 war, the Arabs tried to destabilise Israel through covert infiltration into its territory. This was most effective in the vast empty desert of the Negev and the narrow corridor leading up to Jerusalem. The IDF raised special units to combat this infiltration, among them **Unit 101**, a small formation of fewer than sixty volunteers trained for night fighting. After only four months, Unit 101 was disbanded, but its men were incorporated into the first IDF parachute regiment, the 890th, which led to the formation of an airborne brigade, the **202nd Parachute Brigade**. It fought in the now famous Battle of Mitla Pass in October 1956 and became the spearhead of every action in the later wars that Israel fought against the Arabs.

During the subsequent years, Arab marauders increased their activities and special anti-guerrilla units were formed. Especially effective was the Shaked (Almond) reconnaissance unit. Shaked became the first mobile *Sayeret* (reconnaissance company), organised in six teams, each of five men and a driver led by an officer. Shaked was also the first *Sayeret* to operate with helicopters in terrorist pursuit. While Shaked became masters of the desert, few real commando raids were launched and in order to keep the men's motivation high a special hit squad was formed, known as Shefifon (Rattlesnake). These men, handpicked and trained for their task, became the nucleus of the special hit squads, later performing missions for IDF Intelligence. After the 1967 Six Day War, several *Sayeret* were raised, one in each of the territorial commands. Apart from these they included Shaked, Charuv (Carob), specialising in unconventional warfare in the Jordan Valley, and Egoz (Walnut) in the north. In the 1968–70 War of Attrition, all *Sayeret* fought in deep penetration raids and during the 1973 Yom Kippur War – a high-intensity war fought mainly by armoured forces – the special forces fought mainly in their traditional role of reconnaissance and anti-commando missions. Most of the older *Sayeret* were disbanded after the war, but every regular brigade in the IDF has since raised its own elite reconnaissance.

Sayeret Golani

Formed in 1959, the brigade's reconnaissance company attracted NCOs and volunteers from the ranks of the brigade's battalions to form the Flying Leopards unit. Applicants underwent a gruelling acceptance course to train for their task. Over the years, the **Golani Brigade** or 1st Infantry Brigade, has become not only the IDF's most senior formation but also its premier elite unit, fighting in every war.

Sayeret Golani fought its first combat in a raid on Syrian mortar positions at Tewfiq on the Golan Heights in January 1960. Several more actions of this kind followed, in which the Golani earned its spurs. In the 1967 war, the company fought with the rest of the Golani Brigade assaulting the Golan Heights at the notorious Syrian redoubt at Tel Fahar. During the War of Attrition it fought first in the Lebanese 'Fatahland' against PLO guerrillas and later in the Gaza Strip. The climax of *Sayeret* Golani came during the latter stages of the 1973 Yom Kippur War, when it fought up the slopes of Mount Hermon, losing its commander and its best officers in battle. When the IDF invaded Lebanon in June 1982, *Sayeret* Golani led the way in capturing Beaufort Castle on top of the River Litani gorge in a daring and costly night assault, once again losing its leader. Since then it has spent month after month fighting Hizbullah in South Lebanon in the brutal eighteen-year anti-guerrilla war.

Parachute Reconnaissance (*Sayeret*)

The first Israeli parachute volunteers were trained in Czechoslovakia in 1948. The first IDF parachute unit was formed on Mount Carmel in 1949. The Parachute Recon. (*Sayeret*) was raised in 1955, on the formation of the first (202nd) Parachute Brigade. Many of its volunteers came from Unit 101 and later 890th Parachute Battalion, in which they had been incorporated. The Recon. fought several anti-terrorist actions before the 1956 Sinai Campaign, in which it excelled as a separate unit for the first time in the savage night battle at Mitla Pass.

In 1964 the 35th Parachute Brigade was formed, renumbered from the 202nd, which received the number of a newly formed battalion. The Brigade Recon. became the cream of the new elite formation. Highly trained in all aspects, from parachuting to commando tactics, the brigade fought in the brutal battles around Rafa Junction in 1967, led by the recon. company in halftracks. The *Sayeret* reached its most daring climax during the War of Attrition, where it performed some of the most dangerous commando raids, including deep penetration into Egypt over 300 km from the Israeli lines. During the Yom Kippur War the Parachute Recon. worked with the brigade during the gruelling battles in the Sinai, crossing the

A special forces commando group study their map during an exercise. (IDF via Col D Eshel)

A Sayeret soldier armed with a short barrelled M16 commando-type weapon. (IDF via Col D Eshel)

An IDF SF patrol in Lebanon. The officer in front has a short barrel M16 and a PRC-25 radio. (IDF via Col D Eshel)

An IDF paratroop ambush, the man in the middle has an FN MAG, the others M16A1/s. (IDF via Col D Eshel)

Parachute Recon. Equipment and Training

Early paratroops wore camouflage combat dress, and for ceremonial occasions dark green smocks and trousers and a maroon beret with the infantry badge displayed over a red cloth patch. The parachute insignia is in silver with distinctive coloured cloth underneath signifying qualification: blue for regular, white for instructor and red for combat jumps. In combat paras wear green battle fatigues, protective AC-M Battle Pouches, bullet-resistant vests and the Kevlar A Helmet. The main weapon is the Galil 5.56 mm SAR, but paratroops are trained to operate all sorts of weapons, including enemy equipment.

The Parachute Recon. is normally organised into three platoons/troops, a support group and company HQ, but this varies according to mission profile. Selection and training is similar to the *Sayeret* Golani, but more emphasis is placed on parachute training, night jumps and commando skills.

Sayeret Matkal Equipment

There is very little concrete information about the organisation of the unit, and even its insignia remain mysterious, although members proudly wear their winged emblem. They wear normal paratroop uniform when off duty, but in combat they could use combat wear of all kinds, even civilian turtleneck sweaters and wool skullcaps. On commando missions, the men would wear all kinds of protective clothing. Individual weapons include the Mini-Uzi 9 mm SMG and the new IMI Tavor MTAR (Micro-Tavor Assault Rifle).

Suez Canal and fighting against the Egyptian A-Saiqa on both banks. In June 1976 it took part in the famous Entebbe rescue operation. During the 1982 Lebanon War, the paras fought again in Lebanon, landing by amphibious transports on the Awali River, and fighting some gruelling actions against stubborn PLO resistance while advancing towards Beirut. Since the war the Parachute Recon. has fought Hizbullah guerrillas almost incessantly for eighteen years.

Sayeret Matkal (GHQ Recon.)

This highly secret unit has released very little reliable information about its organisation, activity and training. Commonly referred to as **Unit 269**, or General Staff Reconnaissance, the unit has performed some highly daring missions over the years since its formation in the late 1960s when it was formed as a special commando force under the GHQ Intelligence Corps. Its candidates are hand-picked, and although a small unit, it has developed a remarkable number of senior officers, including at least two chiefs of staff, several major-generals and two prime ministers!

In 1972 the unit stormed the hijacked Sabena airliner at Lod Airport, killing four Black September terrorists and rescuing the passengers. The following month, it mounted a classic commando operation in Lebanon and kidnapped five senior Syrian intelligence officers in an effort to trade them for three captive Israeli pilots. In April 1973 it led a daring coup into the PLO stronghold in downtown Beirut and killed top-ranking PLO officials in retaliation for the Munich

Good close-up of an IDF SF FN MAG gunner engaging a target. Behind him is an Israeli-modified M60 main battle tank, known as the MAGACH, with Blazer ERA (refractive armour) and a 12.7 mm M2 machine-gun over the 105 mm M68 tank gun. (IDF via Col D Eshel)

An SF soldier aiming the Israeli Gill/Spike fibre-optically guided anti-tank missile system, which was first seen publicly in 1999. (Col D Eshel)

Olympics murders. In 1976 the unit led the Entebbe rescue, losing their leader as the only fatality, while storming the compound. These are only a few of the more famous operations which have received wider publicity, but many remain obscure even today.

Sayeret Matkal combines regular conscripts and reservists in its ranks. The unit seems to operate on the A-team basic formation used by the US Delta Force and UK SAS with its own special combat doctrine developed through trial-and-error experience. It is officially under command of the Intelligence Branch, but its commander can answer directly to the Chief of Staff.

The Israeli Police Border Guard

Also called Green Police (as distinct from the regular blue-uniformed civil police) the **Border Guards** are an elite force, operating as a semi-military and highly professional element in anti-terrorist and special operations within the borders of Israel and its occupied territories. The overall strength is about 8,000, 12 per cent of which are recruited from ethnic minorities in Israel, such as Bedouin, Christians, Muslims and mostly Druse. A high proportion are regulars, although recently conscripts have also been recruited.

The Guard operates two special units, both highly professional in their anti-terrorist task, rating among the foremost in the world. The first is called **YAMAM** – the Counter Terrorist/Hostage-Rescue Unit. Set up in

1974 it has made headlines in its spectacular anti-terrorist and hostage-rescue work. The second unit, called **YAMAS**, is an undercover unit, until recently kept highly secret. It was raised during the Intifada uprising and conducts special undercover operations against hardcore terrorists in the West Bank. The **YAMAS** is working closely with IDF undercover units Shimshon and Duvdevan, and in combined efforts, using the General Security Services intelligence, and lately with Palestinian Authority security co-operation, has scored significant success against Hamas leaders, reducing the notorious suicide bomber threat against Israeli civilians.

The Naval Commando (13th Flotilla)

The **Naval Commando**, or **Flotilla 13**, is the oldest special forces unit in the IDF. Similar to global naval commando units like the US Navy SEALs, the British SBS and the German *Marine Kampfschwimmer* unit, Flotilla 13 rates among the best of its kind due to its combat experience and versatility. Its history dates back to the Second World War, when in 1941 two Palestinian Jews serving in the British Marine Commando blew up the Corinth Bridge. A few years later, defying the British blockade of Palestine, a special naval section of the *Palmach* carried out daring underwater sabotage acts, sinking British transports in Haifa port. These men were the forerunners of what was to emerge soon after the creation of the State of Israel as the Naval Commando in Israel's fledgling navy. Using makeshift equipment IDF underwater swimmers went on to sink a Syrian arms transport in Italy and later managed to sink the Egyptian Navy flagship *Emir Farouk* off Gaza in 1948. During the 1973 Yom Kippur War the Naval Commando harassed Egyptian and Syrian ports, virtually stripping the entire region south of Suez bare of enemy shipping. In the continuous anti-guerrilla campaign in Lebanon, it has participated in combined sea and ground actions.

Naval Commando Equipment and Training

The Naval Commando wears white dress uniform when on ceremonial occasion or leave. On duty standard fatigues are worn. The headgear is a dark blue Navy beret with the gold metal Navy insignia over a light blue patch. The commando insignia comprise a winged hat worn with red black cloth underneath. As all commandos are para-jump qualified they wear the silver parachute wings over their right pocket. For underwater combat a specially designed black neoprene rubber diving suit as well as a dark green or grey neoprene equipment vest are donned.

Much of the commando's specialist equipment is locally designed and adapted to the specifications required by the unit. Most of it is still highly confidential and not released. Standard weapons, though, are the AK-47, the 9 mm Uzi, M26 fragmentation grenades and the Belgian 3.3 in Bazooka. But a wide range of weapons is used by the unit on its covert operations, some certainly of exotic nature.

Candidates for Naval Commando service are all volunteers who undergo a stringent examination for physical and mental stamina. The initial indoctrination course covers the basic paratroop/infantry style and concludes with para-qualification for all graduates. Then follows more specialist training including advanced combat swimming, underwater operations, SCUBA diving, assault combat, firearms proficiency, underwater demolition work and intelligence gathering.

| 1948 | 1956 | 1967 | | |
| 1973 | | | | |

campaign ribbons

OT HAGVURA (highest order)

OT HAOZ

OT HAMOFET

DECORATIONS

Zahal INFANTRY UNITS

Paratrooper Commando Wings

Paratrooper (combat jump)

Master paratrooper

Parachute instructor

Paratrooper (free jump)

Paratroopers' wings, metal 1953 onwards

Paratroopers' wings 1949/50 (cloth)

British parachute wings

Naval commando

Senior paratrooper 1949/50 (cloth)

ABOVE: **An Israeli Border Guard in full riot gear.** *(Col D Eshel)*

INSET: ·
Excellent close-up of an Israeli SF, using the IMI Tavor short-barrelled version CTAR 21. *(Col D Eshel)*

ABOVE: *A Sayeret soldier armed with a short-barrelled M16 commando-type weapon.* (IDF via Col D Eshel)

ABOVE: *Part of a Sayeret Golani combat team in action. Both are armed with 5.56 mm GALIL assault rifles (on the left is the long-barrelled version, on the right the short-barrelled). Note also the Golani shoulder flash not normally worn on fatigues.* (Col D Eshel)

LEFT: *There is snow in the depths of winter in the mountains, so snowsuites and climbing gear are needed by some IDF commandos. This one carries an M16A1 assault rifle.* (Col D Eshel)

41

Italy

Italy was the first nation to see the full military potential of airborne troops and began experimenting with them in the mid-1920s. This was largely due to General Giulio Douhet, known as the 'father of strategic air power', whose theories on the command of the air (he wrote *Il Dominio dell'Aria* in 1921) included the use of airborne troops. Five years later the Italians held their first practice drop demonstration at Cinisello and in 1928 formed their first company of trained military paratroopers. By 1930 there were complete battalions trained in parachuting which later became the **Folgore** and **Nembo Divisions** of the Second World War.

Since the war, the Folgore Parachute Brigade has been based at Pisa as a permanent part of the Italian Field Army. There is a parachute infantry regiment of two battalions, plus a *Carabinieri* battalion, an artillery battalion, an aviation flight, an engineer company, a signal company and normal administrative support units. All are parachutable or air-portable.

The airborne *Carabinieri* also have a history going back to the war, but were disbanded in March 1942 and not reformed again until the postwar years (1951). In 1975 the unit was officially named the Tuscánia 1st Airborne *Carabinieri* Battalion and integrated into the Folgore Airborne Brigade. As well as their airborne role they have been involved in fighting organised crime such as the Mafia and have several companies equipped with armoured personnel carriers. Tuscánia *paracadutisti* are also trained in anti-terrorist and anti-guerrilla warfare and have operated, for example, against the Red Brigade. They have also been used on UN peace-keeping missions.

Two marines from the San Marco Marine Battalion, carrying out some 'Hearts & Minds' in Albania. The photograph gives a good close-up of their cap and arm badges. (Stato Maggiore Marina)

A machine-gunner of the Folgore Parachute Brigade prepares to fire his Beretta AR70/90 (light machine-gun model) on its bipod. Note the detachable carrying handle on the top of the MG body. (Stato Maggiore Della Difesa)

Excellent shot of two paratroopers from the Folgore Parachute Brigade, using a digital goniometer for measuring target ranges. The photograph provides a good close-up of their Beretta SCP 90 which is the shorter, lighter version of the 5.56 mm AR70/90 assault rifle. (Stato Maggiore Della Difesa)

Some of the logistic support for the San Marco Marine Group which includes Iveco VM 90 light lorries (at rear) and one of their three logistic ships. (Stato Maggiore Marina)

A spectacular photograph of Comsubin divers being picked up by Italian Navy heavy helicopters (SH-3D Sea Kings) after a mission. Volunteers for this elite force mainly come from the San Marco Marine Battalion. (Stato Maggiore Della Difesa)

Originating in the north of Italy, the **Alpini Brigades** are among the high prestige units of the Italian Army. Basically they are light infantry units, trained and equipped for fighting in the mountains. Since the war there have been five *Brigata Alpina*: Taurinese, Orobica, Tridentina, Cadore and Julia, which are organised with one mountain infantry regiment of three or four battalions, a mountain artillery regiment, signals and engineer companies, an aviation flight, a parachute platoon and administrative units which contain mules as well as vehicles in their supply columns. All are mountain-trained.

The **Raggruppamento Anfibio San Marco** has a history stretching back to the early eighteenth century, and is now part of the *Terza Divisione Navale de la Marina Militare*. After the Second World War (in which towards the end it fought alongside the British on the Cassino front) it was reduced steadily down to battalion size until 1999, when it was decided to enlarge it to brigade status. It now comprises an HQ and command element, three battalions, a logistic group, and a training group, in all some 2,000 men. They form part of the Italian Rapid Intervention Force (FIR) and have their own landing vessels (LCMs and American LVTP-7 tracked amphibians) and fast patrol craft. Their mission would be to spearhead any attack over a hostile beach, then to advance and infiltrate behind enemy lines. They have a wide range of armaments and their battlefield transport includes infantry AFVs. Based at Brindisi, they have three support vessels with floodable docks in the stern

which can accommodate two LCMs (two more are carried elsewhere). They can also call upon the aircraft carrier C 551 *Giuseppe Garibaldi* which can transport some twenty SH Sea King helicopters (to be replaced by the EH-101 in due course).

The **Commando Raggruppamento Subacqui ed Incursori (Comsubin)** is the 200-man elite unit of the Italian Navy which has its roots in the Italian naval assault divers of both world wars. Based at the Varignano naval base near La Spezia, the unit is divided into three groups for operational purposes: the **Gruppo Operativo Incursori (GOI)**; the **Gruppo Operativo Subacqui (GOS)** and the **Gruppo Navale Speciale (GNS)**. GOI comprises combat divers, who use Zodiac-type inflatables, kayaks, submarines etc., and can also be helidropped or parachuted into their objective. GOS is defensive, its main task being to guard naval installations. GNS provides the logistic and technical support for GOI and GOS.

Comsubin personnel have taken part in operations all over the world in recent times, such as Lebanon, Gulf, Rwanda, Somalia, Albania and the former Yugoslavia. Volunteers for this elite force come mainly from the San Marco Marine Battalion and must complete a rigorous ten-month training programme which includes parachuting, demolition and weapons training, hand-to-hand combat, etc. For those who want to serve as combat divers in the GOI group, a further ten-month course must be completed successfully.

A combat patrol from the San Marco Marine Battalion in front of their OTOBREDA Infantry AFV (VCC-2) which is the Italian-built version of the M113 with applique armour on the front and sides, plus an externally mounted 12.7 M2 HB machine-gun which has lateral armoured protection for the gunner. (Stato Maggiore Marina)

Jordan

The Hashemite Kingdom of Jordan has a long tradition of maintaining some of the best-motivated and most highly skilled soldiery in the Middle East. The cream of the Royal Jordanian Army are its special forces. They are the most loyal troops to the royal household and King Abdullah commanded the **Royal Jordanian Special Operations Command** before he succeeded his father, King Hussein, in early 1999.

The modern Jordanian special forces trace their history back to April 1963 when the first jump-qualified paratroops received their coveted wings. A company-sized force was recruited from hand-picked volunteers, mostly from the loyal Bedouin who have personal tribal relations with the royal household. Already of battalion size, the SOC fought Palestinian guerrilla forces during the Black September crisis in 1970 in Amman and at Wachdat, where they routed them in bloody clashes. In 1971 the **Special Forces Brigade** was formed. Its forces clashed once more with Palestinian guerrillas of the PFLP and foiled an attempt to seize the Intercontinental Hotel in Amman in 1976.

Jordan's counter-terrorist unit is the **SOU 71**. It undergoes joint training with the world's best anti-terrorist forces, such as 22 SAS, the US 1st SOF, and the French GIGN, as well as with friendly counter-terrorist teams in Arab countries, such as Egypt, Oman and Bahrain. So far it is not known whether joint training has already taken place with the highly experienced IDF counter-terrorist units, although close co-operation seems to exist.

There is also a Royal Jordanian Air Force **Special Operations Squadron** commanded by King Abdullah's younger brother Prince Faisal.

Soldier from the Jordanian SF wearing his shemag head-dress and carrying a Colt M4 5.56 mm Carbine, the lightweight version of the M16A2. (MPL International Ltd)

Equipment and Training

The uniform of the para/commando units are US woodland-pattern camouflage fatigues, ALICE web gear and M1 helmet. The counter-terrorist unit wears dark blue uniform.

Para/commando units are equipped with M16A2 assault rifles, the Steyr Sniper rifle, and M60 MG and M203 grenade launchers. The anti-terrorist unit is equipped with British DMP-pattern bullet-proof vests, H&K MP5 SMGs, 12-gauge shotguns, and Browning Hi-power automatics.

Training includes sniper skills, explosives and demolition, heliborne operations assault training and special night assault training.

A soldier wearing the new Jordanian SF Gore-tex clothing, aiming his Colt M4 Carbine, which has a lightweight telescoping butt. (MPL International Ltd)

South Korea

South Korea's first special forces were parachute troops assigned to the United Nations partisans during the Korean War, a highly secret guerrilla unit which operated behind the North Korean lines for the purposes of raiding, sabotage and intelligence-gathering. By 1958 this unit was incorporated into the **1st Airborne Infantry Regiment**. Then in 1972 with American training and assistance the Republic of Korea (ROK) Army formed their own special forces unit, beginning with **1st** and **5th Parachute Brigades** and three **ranger battalions**. Some of these units then went on to serve alongside their US counterparts in Vietnam. In the mid-1970s Korean ranger units and the two airborne brigades were converted to special forces brigades. This expansion continued for some years, triggered by the uneasy truce between the two rival Korean states.

Currently, in addition to the Special Warfare HQ and Command there are the **1st, 3rd, 5th, 7th, 9th, 11th** and **13th Special Forces Brigades**, organised on the lines of their US equivalents, with whom they train intensively. At the Special Warfare School near Seoul, parachute, HALO, SCUBA and other specialised training is given, as well as ranger training conducted at the ROK Infantry School. Each infantry division has a reconnaissance battalion, members of which are airborne- and ranger-qualified.

Other airborne-qualified units include the **ROK Marine Reconnaissance Battalion, Navy Combat Swimmers (UDT), Air Force Combat Control and Para-rescue**. These ROK special forces units are capable of operating behind enemy lines or carrying out more conventional operations from within their own territory. The usual allocation of the special forces is one battalion to each Army corps.

The **707th Special Missions Battalion** is the prime counter-terrorist unit, which like so many other formations worldwide came into being following the Palestinian murder of Israeli athletes at the 1972 Munich Olympic Games. By the time of the 1988 Seoul Olympics the 707th had expanded into a 200-strong force, being split into two companies, each organised into four fourteen-man operations teams, with specialist and support teams for back-up. It is also reported that the 707th maintains a group of combat-qualified female operators for use in situations where a man would be suspect. The 707th is based at Songham, southeast of Seoul.

Training for the unit is stringent and vigorous; applicants must come from elsewhere in the special warfare organisation and have already undergone a year-long general special forces course before volunteering for the 707th. Following selection all members are then SCUBA and parachute trained, along with other specialist training and techniques.

The unit has close links with US special forces, including 1st SFOD and SEAL Team Six.

The 707th uses a wide variety of foreign and locally produced weapons, including Colt .45 and Daewoo 9 mm pistols, the H&K MP5 submachine-gun, Daewoo K1 and K2 assault rifles, and H&K PSG1, M24 7.62 mm and RAI .50 sniper rifles.

Equipment and Training

Following the usual arduous physical and psychological selection tests, volunteers undergo a severe basic training course lasting a year, which includes both weapon and parachute training. All ROK special forces troops must also reach black-belt standard in Tae-Kwon-Do or a comparable martial art. They are also trained in tough, realistic exercises for dangerous missions along the Demilitarised Zone such as clearing North Korean tunnels, and they have been used as pursuit units when North Korean raiders have infiltrated into the South.

The normal uniform is a camouflage combat suit. The special forces distinguishing mark is a black beret with the silver SF badge. Weapons and personal equipment are both of US and indigenous origin.

Men of the 707th Special Missions Battalion, South Korea's prime counter-terrorist unit, prepare to assault a practice building. (Specialforces.net)

Lebanon

Following a complete reformation of the Lebanese armed forces after the 1989 Taif Agreement, the Lebanese Army now includes several special forces units. American military advisory experts have been dominant in retraining the new army and Western equipment has replaced the obsolete arsenal which among others included substantial IDF weapons and equipment handed to the Maronite militias, which have been disbanded.

The origins of Lebanon's special forces lie in the 1920s, when the French mandate formed the *Troupes Spéciales du Levant* in Syria and Lebanon. In the 1950s the first commando battalion was formed. During the years of the civil war, most of the regular Lebanese forces disintegrated and sectarian militias grew out of the various religious parties throughout Lebanon. Perhaps the strongest among the Christian Maronites were the Lebanese Forces, the pro-Syrian Maradas, the pro-Western Tigers and the Ketab Phalangists. For a while they were fighting with each other but they later concentrated their efforts against the Palestinians, gaining substantial Israeli military assistance. Among the elite units was the **101st Parachute Company**, which received jump training from the Israelis and a ranger unit, which was raised with Western assistance after the 1982 war.

Two new commando units have been established (perhaps within the present ORBAT). The first is the **Red Beret** airborne element which is of battalion strength. The unit was trained by Western advisors

Equipment and Training
Until recently Lebanese special forces uniforms and equipment still related to the militia era, and IDF standard combat uniforms and weapons could be seen throughout. But the reform of the Lebanese armed forces has now replaced these with mostly Western-pattern uniforms and weapons. The red beret is the standard special forces headgear and is worn in the French manner, with the insignia over the right eye. The **marine commandos** however, wear a light blue beret in British style with the insignia over the left eye.

Individual weapons include the FN Browning 9 mm M1935, Walther P38 and Commander Colt Pistols, MAT 49, Sterling L2A3(Mk4) SMG, 7.5 mm MAS M 1949/56 assault rifles and the AK-47 Kalashnikov.

A two-month ranger course under US Army Ranger disciplines is conducted. Training includes six weeks' physical training, underwater demolition and anti-guerrilla work including special urban warfare.

from the USA and the UK. Reports indicate that elements of this force have seen action against Hizbullah in the Syrian-controlled Beka'a Valley in 1997 and recently in the Dinnieh hills fighting Islamic terrorists of the Wahabi sect. There is also a newly raised Lebanese **marine commando** unit trained by British Royal Marine Commando and US Navy SEAL instructors.

Libya

Currently Libya fields no fewer than nineteen para/commando battalions in its military organisation. Another formation, the **Republican Guard**, can also be regarded as a special forces unit. This is according to best reports of brigade strength. There seems to be a **naval commando unit**,

equipped with six mini-submarines of the Yugoslav-made R-2 Mala Class and some fast craft. Training is mainly by Russian instructors, and most of the equipment is Russian, though as of late Libya has been purchasing Western equipment as well.

Morocco

Until 1956 Moroccan soldiers served in French Army units, including their special forces. Today there are currently two **paratroop** brigades and six **commando** battalions in service. The **Royal Guard**, which consists of one battalion and two cavalry squadrons, can also be regarded as special forces.

During the 1973 Yom Kippur War, a formation of

Moroccan para commandos fought under Syrian command against the Israelis, on the slopes of Mount Hermon in the Golan Heights. During 1976 Moroccan special forces fought Mauritanian forces in Western Sahara and against the Polisario around Bir Enzaran. In April 1977 three Moroccan commando units were in action in Zaire.

The Netherlands

Holland was for many years one of the major sea powers of the world, so its marines have a long and honourable history stretching back to their formation in 1665 as the Royal Dutch Navy Infantry Corps. Over the centuries they have lived up to their motto *Quo patet orbis* ('As far as the world extends') and seen action world wide, such as against the British in North America in the late seventeenth century, when they re-captured New Amsterdam (New York) and held it until 1692. Ten years later, however, some 400 Dutch marines supported the British in capturing Gibraltar and they have maintained friendly co-operation ever since. Dutch marines also fought in China during the Boxer Rebellion of 1900, and in the Dutch East Indies after the Second World War, when they re-established Dutch rule after the Japanese occupation.

After Indonesia became independent in 1949, the Royal Dutch Marines returned home and were reorganised as the **Koninklijk Nederlands Korps Mariniers (KNKM)** (now just over 3,000 men in total) which was then put under NATO command. In 1973 a special amphibious force the United Kingdom/Netherlands Amphibious Force (UKNLAF) was formed. The two main components of this force are the Amphibious Task Group (basically the ships) and the Landing Force (the UKNLLF) which comprises the men of 3 Commando Brigade, RM and of the Dutch Group of Operational Units Marines (GOUM). The KNKM provides units for this force, such as its **1st Marine Battalion** and **7 Troop SBS (NL)**. The total Netherlands contribution to the UKNLLF is some 1,100 men, which includes in addition to the marine battalion, indirect fire support, landing craft, air defence, reconnaissance, engineer and logistical assets. Its light infantry units, which are rapidly deployable, are all amphibious-trained and capable of operating anywhere in the world.

The 7 Troop SBS (NL) is comparable with the UK Royal Marines SBS, its Dutch name being *Amfibisch Verkennings Peloton*, and it comprises twenty-five all ranks, who are all paratroop-trained combat swimmers. During wartime it would be used for such missions as gathering intelligence, sabotage, etc., but in peacetime it is responsible for security on board Dutch oil-rigs, ferries and other civilian vessels. GOUM is based at barracks in Doorn, whilst other smaller elements of the KNKM are deployed in the Dutch Antilles at the naval base of Paera.

Bijzondere Bijstands Eenheid (BBE)

Another important element of the Dutch marines is the **BBE**, their counter-terrorist unit, which contains some ninety highly trained volunteers divided into three platoons, which are again subdivided into five-man teams. It specialises in anti-terrorist/hostage-taking situations, and also contains the usual array of experts such as snipers, demolition men, etc. A typical example of the use of the BBE was in May 1977, when a group of South Moluccan extremists took over a school then hijacked a train between Rotterdam and Groningen. On 11 June, whilst a pair of Dutch Air Force jets made a supersonic run over the train to distract the extremists, the BBE blew open the train doors, shouted at the hostages to lie down and took on the South Moluccans, killing six and capturing the rest. Only one of the marines was wounded but unfortunately two of the hostages were killed.

Stinger ground-to-air missile team of the Netherlands Air Mobile Brigade get ready to fire their missile. Its high explosive Magnavox fragmentation warhead is highly effective and over 50,000 are in service worldwide. (Patrick Allen)

49

Men of the Netherlands Air Mobile Brigade leaving their helicopter. *(Patrick Allen)*

The BBE co-operates fully with both local police and *gendarmerie* as well as the military. It also maintains close links with such other specialised units as the French GIGN, the German GSG9, the Spanish GEO and in particular the Belgian ESI.

Korps Commandotroepen (KCT)

The present Dutch commando unit can trace its history back to 22 March 1942 when forty-eight Dutchmen from the Royal Brigade Princess Irene began commando training in Achnacarry, Scotland. Eventually twenty-five were awarded the coveted green beret and in June 1942, No. 2 (Dutch) Troop was formed as part of No. 10 (Interallied) Commando. The following year they were deployed against the Japanese in the Far East, but returned to Europe in mid-1944 to take part in Operation *Market Garden*. They won battle honours at Arnhem, Nijmegen, Eindhoven, Vlissingen and Westkappelle all in 1944, to add to Arakan. Later, these battle honours were joined by Djakarta 1948 and Central Sumatra 1948–9 on their Queen's Colour, which was presented by HM Queen Juliana in 1995.

During the 1950s the **KCT** developed into an organisation with three operational companies (104, 105 and 108), a training company and a combat service support company. Operational companies comprised approximately 115 soldiers. Subsequent operations included special Green Beret missions during the Korean War, also in Surinam (1952), New Guinea (1959–60), West Germany (1961–3) and flood disaster rescue operations in Holland in 1953. Expenditure cuts in 1964 led to the three commando companies being replaced by 104 Long Range Reconnaissance and Patrol Company (LRRP).

A Dutch commando of the KCT. Note the size of his bergen, all SF must be able to carry heavy loads as a matter of course. Dutch commandos have been deployed in peace-keeping missions in both Bosnia (1995 and 1998) and Kosovo (1999). (KCT)

In addition to their operational mission of being the eyes and ears of 1 (NL) Corps from 1964 to 1990, they also took on the task of training all combat units on a two-week 'Panterstorm' course, and in this way over 100,000 conscripts and regulars received valuable training. Since the disappearance of the Berlin Wall and the end of the Cold War, the KCT has played a full part in UN operations all over the world, and in 1992, the 11th Airmobile Brigade was formed (see below).

On 1 January 1993, **108 Special Forces Company** was established and deployed as commando-special operations. Then 104 LRRP Company was given reserve status from 1 September 1995, but the size of 108 SF Company clearly needed to be increased in order to cope with world problems such as the situation in Bosnia and, on 1 October 1998, the KCT was expanded once again in a drastic reorganisation. Since then it has consisted of three commando troop companies – 104, 105 and 108, a special forces company, and a staff, support and instruction company. The commando companies are divided into commando teams which are organised, trained and equipped to operate independently for long periods. All are trained for insertion on foot, by vehicle, by helicopter, or by free-fall parachuting (up to 2,000 m).

Companies each have three specially trained teams for insertion in areas that have abundant water (inland waterways) so need diving skills and equipment; in mountainous terrain, so they must be expert climbers and skiers; or by parachute from extreme heights (up to 10,000 m using HALO/HAHO techniques). Each company also has special teams trained in counter-terrorism. Every individual becomes a specialist in a particular skill, so that each commando team consists of two snipers, two demolition experts, two medics and two communications specialists.

Commando training lasts for twelve months in total for serving soldiers who volunteer and fourteen months for those direct from civilian life. This is divided into: preparatory training (either four or twelve weeks), fourteen weeks' basic commando training and twenty-six weeks' advanced commando training. At the end of stage 2 those who have successfully completed the course, which is both physically and mentally demanding, are awarded their coveted green berets at a special ceremony. The final stage of the last twenty-six week training period is geared to operational missions and the skills and drills that go with them. Regular training also includes vehicle driving, combat life saver training, free-fall parachute training, etc. and for the last ten weeks they are additionally trained in their chosen individual skill, as snipers, medics, demolitions experts or communications specialists.

The present KCT is assigned to plan and conduct special operations within the sphere of Allied defence and crisis management and to provide training for units of 1 Ge/NL Army Corps. It performs its major tasks in small, self-contained and self-supporting sub-units that can undertake such missions as special reconnaissance, including searching and surveillance of important military targets in enemy territory or unknown areas, offensive and direct action against high-value targets; military assistance and collateral activities such as combat search and rescue, counter-terrorism, humanitarian assistance and disaster relief. Without a doubt all members of this formidable little force continue to live up to their stirring motto: *Nunc aut nunquam* ('Now or never').

11th Air Mobile Brigade
Operating as part of NATO's Multinational Division (Central), which is part of ARRC, the Netherlands

A realistic casualty is given first aid during an exercise. All SF must be trained in first aid and every small group contains a medic. (KCT)

Dutch Green Berets must be able to operate in the most extreme conditions – such as these mountains (definitely not in Holland). (KCT)

11th Air Mobile Brigade consists of highly trained soldiers who are some of the best in the Dutch armed forces. CH-47D Chinooks enable them to be deployed rapidly, together with the necessary weapons, equipment and supplies. They can also call upon the support of fast-attack helicopters (soon these will be AH-64 Apaches), whilst light all-terrain vehicles, state-of-the-art communications and portable anti-tank weapons give them great flexibility once they have been deposited on the ground. These men are able to deal with all types of emergencies which include, as well as their NATO role, operating under UN auspices – a battalion-sized unit can be deployed at very short notice. During the period January 1994 to July 1995, all three of the battalions were committed in Bosnia as part of the UN Protection Force.

In addition to three infantry battalions there are various support troops, whilst their helicopters belong to the Netherlands Air Force Tactical Helicopter Group. Supporting troops include a heavy mortar company of twelve 120 mm mortars, an engineer company, a maintenance company and a medical company. The Brigade has considerable firepower with its mortars, AA missiles (Stinger), anti-tank missiles (AT-4, TOW and Dragon) etc. Apart from the heavy mortars all weapons are man-portable. Communications are highly sophisticated, as is the use of GPS (Global Positioning System).

The Brigade's history goes back to the 11th Brigade which was formed on 14 November 1960, then five years later became the 11th Mechanized Infantry Brigade, then in 1992, adopted the airmobile role.

This commando sniper has a difficult job to camouflage himself and his weapon in snowy conditions. Note that he also has a 'spotter'. (KCT)

BELOW: *A well camouflaged commando sniper waits in ambush. (KCT)*

RIGHT: *KCT paratroopers take part in the regular NATO and world parachuting competitions. This one was held at Bordeaux between 16–26 March 1998. (KCT)*

New Zealand

The **New Zealand Special Air Service Squadron** was first formed in 1954 to operate with the British 22nd SAS Regiment in the Malayan emergency, but selection and training delayed its actual deployment until the following year. In 1957 the squadron returned home to disband but was reprieved, a single troop being sent to Australia for parachute training. This continued until 1965 and the creation of a parachute training school in New Zealand just outside Auckland. In 1962 a detachment of thirty to forty men was sent to Korat in Thailand to operate with US Army special forces and US Marines in performing reconnaissance missions and training the Thai Rangers in anti-guerrilla warfare. In 1963 the squadron was redesignated **1st SAS Rangers Squadron (SRS)** in commemoration of two famous ranger formations of the Maori Wars.

Over the next two years the Squadron's four detachments were sent in rotating order to Brunei to operate alongside their British counterparts the 22nd SAS Regiment, in the covert war between Indonesia and Malaysia. In November 1968 No. 4 Troop of the SRS was sent to Vietnam, serving as part of an Australian SAS squadron. Thereafter troops from the squadron were rotated in year-long tours that continued in Vietnam until February 1971.

1978 saw another redesignation, from 1st Rangers Squadron to **1st SAS Squadron**. Both the training school and the regiment were now located at the Papakura base. The latest information gives the 1st SAS Group base as at Whenuapai. It consists of five troops, a headquarters and a separate small training establishment. Its task is to support New Zealand defence forces in their operations and, like the SAS in the United Kingdom, it has a major commitment to counter-terrorist operations whenever and wherever they might arise. Most recent operations include a link-up with the Australian SAS to form the ANZAC element of the Allied special forces in the 1991 Gulf War.

Equipment and Training

The uniform is the standard New Zealand Army one, but badges are similar to those of the British SAS. Until 1986 the New Zealand SAS wore maroon berets but now wear the same sand-coloured beret as the British and Australian SAS and the similarity of their badges display their historical connections to those units, with whom they train most regularly. Primary weapons include the M16A2 5.56 mm assault rifle, Heckler & Koch MP5 9 mm submachine-gun and PSG 1.7 sniper rifle, the Remington Mk 870 shotgun and Mk 24 sniper rifle.

Also like their Australian and British counterparts the NZ SAS are schooled in reconnaissance, hostage- and prisoner-recovery from hostile territories, behind-the-lines strategic insertion and attack, as well as guerrilla and counter-insurgency operations. Their training and selection processes are as stringent and exhausting, their pass rate similarly small and their secrecy if anything even deeper, for there has been nothing on the level of Princes Gate to attract the public's gaze. They also train with South-east Asian countries such as Thailand, Indonesia and Singapore.

Norway

Like its neighbours Sweden and Denmark, Norway has both marine commandos and paratroopers as well as special counter-terrorism units in its police. The naval element is the **Marinjegertroppen** a force of some 200 all ranks, which operates in small units of two men upwards. They are naturally experts in Arctic warfare and well able to survive in such conditions for long periods. Their training and equipment is very similar to that of the British SBS and the US SEALs, with whom they have strong links. In time of war, their missions would be deep penetration, reconnaissance and sabotage of enemy naval installations. Volunteers must pass a stringent twenty-two-week course at the naval diving school at Haakonsvern naval station, near Bergen. Their base is the Ramsund naval station in Nordland.

The **Fallskjermjegerkommandoen** – Parachute Ranger Commandos – can trace their history back to the Second World War, when a number of Norwegian Army personnel who had escaped to the UK formed an independent Norwegian company in 1942, which was later made part of the 1st British Airborne Division. In addition to these paratroopers OSS (Office of Strategic Services) saboteurs, who were part of the Norwegian Special Operations Group (OSS), were parachuted into Norway in March 1945 to cut the Nordland Railway and perform other acts of sabotage. After the war all paratroop units were disbanded, but in the early 1960s, interest was revived and a parachute training school was opened at Trandum, near Oslo. Training does not just concentrate on

Norwegian parachute ranger commandos are hand-picked and must pass a gruelling course before becoming fully fledged Fallskjermjegerkommandoen. *This tough-looking quartet in their SCUBA diving gear are about to be dropped by parachute, presumably offshore. (specialforces.net)*

parachuting but also on commando training, so that those who successfully pass the sixteen-week course, are fully trained *Fallskjermjegerkommandoen*. However, it is an exceptionally hard and demanding course, so although the recruits are hand-picked fewer than half of the original applicants pass out. As one might expect, Arctic training is high on the list.

Pakistan

The Pakistan armed forces maintain a **Special Services Group (Navy) (SSG(N))** and a **Special Services Group (Army) (SSG(A)**. The former was first raised in 1967. Midget submarines and chariots were subsequently added in order to increase the reach of frogman operations. In 1991–2, new midget submarines, known as shallow water attack submarines (SWAS), were introduced.

The SSG(N) consists of highly trained, dedicated and motivated men who are multidimensionally trained, so that they are capable of performing almost any mission. The main focus of their training and subsequent operations has been SEAL operations, now with the added dimension of the midget submarines. Commanded by a captain, the group is basically divided into two wings – Midgetarian and SEALs. To achieve a rapid response and enhance their effectiveness, they have been put directly under the Commander Pakistan Fleet (COMPAK).

All members of SSG(N) are volunteers from the Pakistan Navy, who must first undergo aptitude testing and searching interviews before being selected to commence their training. The range of weaponry which they must be able to use is considerable, for example, a midget submarine can carry torpedoes and/or mines (including limpet mines), the exact weapon configuration depending upon the mission. Members of the SEAL group must be proficient with all types of assault weapons (9 mm, 7.62 mm or 5.56 mm), shotguns, rocket launchers, special explosives, laser configured sights, anti-terrorist equipment and various parachute rigs.

Normal camouflage combat suits are worn, their primary distinguishing marks being: a maroon beret with normal naval badge and the silver commando insignia on the left pocket. Of course a wide variety of specialised clothing is also worn, depending on their mission and the terrain in which they are operating.

It is thought that there are some three battalions in the SSG(A), plus an additional independent counter-terrorist company. Tasking of these special forces is in the hands of three top level intelligence bodies – Military Intelligence (MI); Directorate of Inter-Services Intelligence (ISI) and the Intelligence Bureau (IB).

A member of Pakistan's Special Forces, armed with H&K MP5K submachine-gun (and a holstered pistol) wearing a night viewing device. Note also his flak vest, webbing equipment (including magazine pouches, water bottle etc.) also the taped-together double magazine on his SMG. *(High Commission of Pakistan)*

Unarmed combat and martial arts form an important part of SSG training. *(High Commission of Pakistan)*

Important elements of the Pakistan SSG(N) are their midget submarines, known as shallow water attack submarines (SWAS) as seen here. (High Commission of Pakistan)

Pakistan SSG must be fully trained in all types of parachuting, including HAHO and HALO. This group of free-fallers sport some splendid handlebar moustaches! (High Commission of Pakistan)

Philippines

The Philippines first began studying the system of integrating SF operations into their overall defence plan in 1958, when Brigadier-General Ramon L. Cannu, then a captain, was tasked with working with a group of US SF officers, which led on to a core of Philippine Army officers being trained by the 11th US SF Team from Okinawa. The team was assigned to the Philippine Army (PA) on 1 April 1962 and attached to the PA Schools Centre. As a result the **1st SF Company (Airborne), AFP** (Air Forces of the Philippines) was organised on 25 June 1962. US support ended early in 1964 and that summer the **Special Forces Group (Airborne) PA**, was organised as a provisional unit. Two units – A Company 10th BCT (Battalion Combat Team) and the Civic Action Center, 1st Infantry Division, were attached in October 1964 and March 1965 respectively.

More reorganisations followed and the next four years saw the expansion of the unit to a size more responsive to the security demands of the times. In August 1964, the unit was renamed **Home Defense Forces Group (Airborne)** and was then composed of the 1st SF, the Supply Maintenance Platoon and A Company, 10 BCT of the TABAK Infantry Division, PA. During this expansion period more specialised training in parachuting (HALO) and SCUBA diving took place and on 1 July 1967, the group was declared fit and operational. Unfortunately the unit then lost 70 per cent of its personnel who were absorbed into a peacekeeping mission in South Vietnam. In 1970, the group was reduced to company size, but on 31 January 1973 it was once again expanded into a group with five operational companies and one HQ company.

The elements of the SF units (now known as home defence forces units) remained unchanged although there was an alteration in the internal organisation of SF teams, from eleven (two officers and nine men) to fifteen (one officer and fourteen men). Later this was changed to a twelve-man team (one officer and eleven men) so as to be more responsive. The unit was called the Home Defense Forces Group (Airborne) until 16 April 1988, when it was renamed **Special Forces Group (Airborne)**. Finally, on 16 November 1989, it was renamed: **Special Forces Regiment (Airborne)**, PA. The activation of the Special Operations Command, PA, on 1 June 1996, made the SFR(A) one of its subordinate units.

For the past forty years the unit and its predecessors have been a bulwark of the country's unconventional warfare operations, figuring prominently in the liberation of certain settlements. With the demands of changing times it has assumed new roles, which has meant the SFR(A) learning new skills such as human resource development, disaster relief operations, crisis management, environmental protection, computer literacy and other imperatives of a developing country. It has also been chosen as the PA's disaster response task group. Additionally, it has become the first ever Philippines counter-terrorist group and will respond to hostage-taking and similar crises.

The Capabilities of the SFR(A)
These are: to develop, organise, train, equip, command and control indigenous, paramilitary forces; to provide mobile training teams (MTT) to organise, train and advise cadres of conventional forces tasked to administer paramilitary forces; to conduct denial operations to prevent enemy access, influence and control over a particular area of strategic value; to perform PSYOP, civil action operations and humanitarian assistance; to provide strike operations by SF or jointly with indigenous troops; to provide forward air control for air missions; to undertake sabotage, subversion and abduction of selected personnel; and search, rescue and recovery operations.

As with other SF, specialised parachuting (HALO and HAHO) forms an integral part of their normal training. (Public Information Office, GHQ Armed Forces of the Philippines)

Having been dropped by their helicopter, this SFR(A) team practises storming a building. *(Public Information Office, GHQ Armed Forces of the Philippines)*

Watermanship in inflatables is just another part of general training for these Philippine SF. *(Public Information Office, GHQ Armed Forces of the Philippines)*

SF Team Organisation

It is worth taking up some space here to go into detail of the SF team SFR(A) organisation, because it is no doubt the same/very similar to other SF teams worldwide, even though the number of men in a team may vary and the jobs have to be shared out differently. Note that all the weapons mentioned are American in origin.

Position	Responsible for
Team Leader	Planning and supervising unit operations Training, morale and discipline of the men Organisation of activities and operations within given area Equipped with map, compass and binoculars Armed with M653
Team Sgt	Assistant of CO Attends to administrative requirements of the team During training can instruct subjects on ops and intelligence Armed with M16
Asst Team Sgt	Responsible for morale and discipline of men Dive master and underwater operation specialist of the team Armed with M16/M203
Operation Sgt	Responsible for the team's preparation and infiltration to the area of operation Jump Master of team Can train selected paramilitary or guerrilla personnel on operational function Equipped with map, compass, GPS Armed with M16/M203
Intelligence Sgt	Responsible for the co-ordination of the outer and inner security of the team's operational area. Can operate overt and covert intelligence net independently or along with other AFP Units Equipped with silent killing devices Armed with Carbine or M653
Demolition and Explosive Specialist	Responsible for laying mines and booby traps against the enemy The logistic NCO of the team Can instruct subjects on arming and disarming of explosives, placement of mines and booby traps and sabotage operations Equipped with explosives Armed with M16/M203
Asst Demolition & Explosive Specialist	Can instruct subjects on demolition and can function similarly with the demolition specialist Equipped with explosives Armed with M14/M16
Heavy Weapons Specialist	Can instruct subjects on marksmanship, operation, care and maintenance of govt issued FA Armed with M60
Light Weapons Specialist	Can also teach marksmanship and disassembly/reassembly of weapons that are in the inventory of the AFP Armed with M60/Ultimax
Medical Specialist	Responsible for the medical requirements of the team Can teach subjects on first aid, hygiene and sanitation Equipped with M16/M14
Communications Specialist	Responsible for the signals requirements of the team Can instruct subjects on installation or expedient antennas, message writing and continuous wave operations Equipped with radio sets, flashlights, flare gun Armed with M16
Chief Radio Supervisor	Responsible for team radios Can instruct subjects on radio telephone procedures, silent signals and different kinds of guerrilla communications system Equipped with radio sets, flashlights, flare gun Armed with M16

Men of the Philippines Special Forces Regiment during a jungle exercise, which is one of the basic elements of their training. (Public Information Office, GHQ Armed Forces of the Philippines)

59

Poland

Less than ten years ago, the **Grupa Reagowania Operacyjino Mobilnego (GROM)**, or Thunder as it is sometimes called, was formed from volunteers of the many special forces units which had existed in the Cold War era, such as commandos and naval assault swimmers, and already has an enviable reputation. Much of this is due to the hard work and dedication of its commander, Colonel Slawomir Petelicki. Like the British SAS and other SF units, GROM is very security conscious, so it is impossible to discover more than outline details. It is thought that there are some 250–300 operatives, including women, and that all speak at least two languages. Many are paramedics and all are fully trained as combat assault personnel. They operate in four-person teams and have high individual skills in weapons (all training is done using live ammunition) and other abilities.

In 1944, they showed their prowess to the world when they were selected to take part in the American-led invasion of Haiti (Operation *Restore Democracy*) and some fifty-five GROM personnel were sent to train with US 3rd Special Forces Group in Puerto Rico. Subsequently they provided VIP guards for such visitors to the island as UN Secretary General Butros Butros-Ghali and US Secretary of Defense William Perry. They also took part in a hostage-rescue operation, storming a building, putting out a fire and rescuing the hostage without any bloodshed. As a result of their excellent work in Haiti, they were awarded the Army Commendation Medal, the first time that a foreign unit had been commended in this way by the USA. Back in Poland, they had the onerous task of being responsible for safeguarding Pope John Paul II when he visited in 1995.

Polish paratroopers played a considerable part in Allied airborne assaults during the Second World War; the best remembered is perhaps Operation *Market Garden*. The Russians also raised a Polish airborne battalion which took part in reconnaissance missions behind the German lines. After the war it was disbanded, but in 1957, it was re-formed and enlarged to divisional status as the 6th Air Assault division (Pomerania). By 1981, it had been reduced to just two airborne battalions. One of these, the **401st** is trained in LRRP and other special missions.

The 7th Lujcka Naval Assault Brigade is a highly trained elite amphibious force which is tasked with the defence of Poland's coastline and of their Baltic Sea bases. It comprises three mechanised infantry battalions plus supporting weapons, a total of roughly 4,250 men. The mechanised infantry are equipped with such amphibious vehicles as the OT-62C APC.

Polish paratroopers join British and French paras in a C-130 Hercules as they prepare to reenact the D-Day para drop near Ranville, Normandy, fifty years later in June 1994. (MPL International Ltd)

Portugal

The **Portuguese Marine Corps** can trace its history back to 1618 when the Battalion of the Armada of the Crown of Portugal was first formed. Over the next two centuries it played a significant part in Portuguese naval affairs and in the late 1700s became the *Brigada Real de Marinha* (Royal Naval Brigade), which contained over 2,000 marines. It took part in several engagements against the French, in close co-operation with units of the British Royal Navy under Nelson. In 1808 marines accompanied members of the Portuguese Royal Family to Brazil when they were forced to flee during the Napoleonic Wars. In 1822, when Brazil became independent under Dom Pedro son of King João VI of Portugal, they helped form the marine corps of the Brazilian Navy. In more modern times, the marines played an active role in the fighting that took place in their ex-African colonies, Angola, Cape Verde, Guinea and Mozambique. These struggles involved over 12,000 marines between 1961 and 1076 and many medals were awarded for valour.

Since the military coup of 25 April 1974 and the end of the wars in Africa, the role of the armed forces as a whole has changed significantly. Shortly afterwards, on 24 June 1974, the **Commando do Corpo de Fuzileiros (CCF)**, the Marines Corps Command, came into being, comprising: the **Forca de Fuzileiros do Continento (FFC)**, the Marines Force, the **Escola de Fuzileiros (EF)**, the Marines School, and other marine units and craft. According to the latest figures, there are three battalions of marines (two of light infantry and one of naval police), together with a fire support unit, an amphibious equipment support unit, a tactical transport unit and, most importantly, the **Destacamento de Accoes Especiais (DAE)**, Special Actions Detachment. Marines are trained at the Marine School at Vale do Zebro which opened in 1961, whilst the Marine Force is based at the Alfeite naval base near Lisbon.

The Special Actions Detachment is a highly trained, specialised force which resembles the US SFAIs and the RM SBS. They are trained and equipped to undertake such missions as amphibious raids, sabotage, obstacle removal, destruction of enemy vessels etc., as well as humanitarian aid in high-risk areas (e.g. oil-rigs). They receive the type of specialised training necessary for such work which includes working with helicopters, boats (including canoes and kayaks), parachuting, land operations and the usual SF personal training such as weapons and explosives, advanced first aid, personal defence, navigation, evasion and survival.

The landing battalions are supported by a number of naval vessels: three LCTs of the Bombarda type which can carry loads up to 350 tons and six LCM 100s and LCM 400s. Weapons used by the *Fuzileiros* include the tried and tested MP-K machine pistol made by the German company Walther, which is found to stand up to saltwater attack outstandingly well.

According to the latest survey of the Portuguese Army, there is also one airborne brigade, two commando battalions and one special operations company, so within a small army of some 25,650, a fair proportion of troops are concerned with SOF. Although interest in parachuting in Portugal began in the 1920s, the first unit, which became known as the **21st** *Batalho Cacadores Para-que-distas* (BCP) – Light Infantry Battalion – was not formed until 1956 as part of the Portuguese Air Force. Thereafter, like the Marines they played an active part in the struggles in Africa, until 1975, when all disbanded BCP units came together to form the *Corpo de Fropas Para-que-distas* (CTP), Paratroops Corps. In 1993, the Paratroops Corps was disbanded and the following year, the *Brigada Para-que-distas Independente* (BPI), Independent Airborne Brigade, came into being in the Portuguese Army, bringing together paratroopers from both Air Force and Army. The *Commando de Tropas Aero Transportadas* (CTAT), Airborne Command, was formed at the same time, based at Trancos.

In 1994, the BPI became part of the NATO ARRC. Since then all three of its airborne battalions have served with IFOR in Bosnia. Members of the BPI wear a distinctive green beret.

Russia

Pick up any book about elite special forces of the Cold War era and you are bound to find a section on the highly trained and highly secretive *Spetsnaz* units – **Voiska Spetsialnoje Naznachienie (VSN)**, Forces of Special Designation – which had no real equivalent on the Western side of the Iron Curtain. Their main purpose was known as 'diversionary reconnaissance' (*diversiya rezvedka*) which meant that they would have been sent in ahead of the main assaulting force to sabotage vital Western installations (e.g. nuclear weapons sites), to lay mines so as to disrupt counter-attacks, to mark suitable landing sites and generally to prepare the ground for the much larger follow-up force. This was of course never put into practice in Europe, but one of the most recent occasions when these forces were actually used was spearheading the invasion of Afghanistan in 1979.

Despite the fact that the Cold War has long ended, such specialised troops still remain within the Russian Federation armed forces and in those of many of the former Soviet republics, although their roles have somewhat changed. Now they are far more likely to be used in SAS-type roles, although judging from their moderate performance in places like Chechnya they are clearly not as well trained as they were in the bad old days. Nevertheless, it would be foolish to discount their abilities. They have also come out of the shadows to a degree, now being officially recognised as part of the Russian Federation armed forces, so they wear identifying badges whereas in the past they all wore standard airborne uniforms and insignia. Their training, like that of all SF is intensive and far tougher than that of the normal Russian conscript.

Current *Spetsnaz* units are:

• Razvedchiki – one battalion divided into two companies (one for LRRP and one for airborne operations)

- Rejdoviki – a brigade-sized formation which operates in battalion- or company-sized units in an independent reconnaissance role
- Vysotniki – a brigade-sized formation operating in small units of eleven men each, the closest equivalent to British SAS or US SF

There are still **Naval *Spetsnaz*** brigades serving in all four of the main Russian naval fleets (Northern, Baltic, Black Sea and Pacific) and, whilst little is known about their activities, they are probably understrength and less well motivated than before. Naval *Spetsnatz* must learn all the requisite underwater skills as well as how to operate the specialised equipment and weapons which go with their amphibious reconnaissance role.

Mention has been made in the press of the crack Russian ***Omon*** (also called *Omsn* or *Osnaz*) force, whose name means 'black berets', being used in Chechnya and suffering casualties during some of their operations. *Omon* are believed to be specialised troops raised by the Ministry of Internal Affairs for hostage-rescue/security operations. In past campaigns, such as in Afghanistan in December 1980, they were generally credited with attacking the presidential palace in Kabul and murdering the President and his family. More recently they have also been used against criminal gangs, drug barons and the like, many of whom hail from Chechnya or have links with the Chechen guerrillas. *Omon* members undergo a ten-month training programme, which starts with unarmed combat and fitness training, progressing on to hostage-rescue scenarios, using dummy aircraft and/or buildings, etc. The Ministry of the Interior also has special anti-terrorism troops known as the Kondor Division.

The nearest thing to Royal Marine commandos in the Russian Federation Navy are the ***Morskaya Pekhota*** – Marine Infantry – which are classified as 'guards' units, being an honorific title given to elite units. There are three divisions (103, 104 and 105) and they are comprised of a mixture of volunteers and specially selected 'top grade' conscripts. Training is rigorous, with the emphasis on physical training. Units are based around the battalion battle group, which contains motorised infantry and supporting arms – artillery, engineers, etc., including frogmen. They are trained to operate in advance of an amphibious landing. Their normal combat dress is black denims, with a black beret or black steel helmet. Like the Royal Marines, they operate using specialised, purpose-built craft, from small rubber boats to large ocean-going LPDs.

*Spetsnatz **soldiers take time out from operations in Afghanistan to indulge in some karate.*** (MPL International Ltd)

A Spetsnatz *patrol, led by a tracker dog and his handler, working with the frontier force during the war in Afghanistan.* (MPL International Ltd)

A Spetsnatz *patrol scrambling down a slope during the Afghanistan conflict. They are armed with AK-47 Kalashnikov automatic rifles and led by a tracker dog team.* (MPL International Ltd)

With his Kalashnikov AKM at the ready, a Spetsnaz Spetsrota *counter-terrorist soldier from the Felixdzerzhinsky Division, leaps through a window during a living firing exercise in the unit's training village. An instructor waits inside to the right, to monitor his pupils' progress.* (MPL International Ltd)

A patrol from the Spetsnaz, the Soviet special forces, moves across a snow field during operations along the Russian border with Finland. They are armed with AK-74 5.45 mm Kalashnikov automatic rifles. (MPL International Ltd)

A Russian paratrooper from the 106th Guards Airborne Division, fires his AK-74 Kalashnikov assault rifle on the tactical ranges near Moscow. (MPL International Ltd)

This close-up of Russian marine infantry Morskaya Pekhota *gives a good view of their black uniform, black berets, distinctive badges, etc. (Col D Eshel)*

This Spetsnatz *patrol in Afghanistan finds time to make a fuss of their tracker dog. (MPL International Ltd)*

Saudi Arabia

There are two airborne/airmobile battalions grouped into a **Special Forces Brigade** in the Saudi forces. Furthermore there are three special forces companies with parachute training and a Royal Guards regiment with three battalions. In July 1961 about a company-strength battle group entered Kuwait to assist 42 Royal Marine Commando during a crisis there. It was the first time that Saudi special forces had operated outside their territory.

The organisation of paratroop forces, like the rest of the armed forces, is rather confused, due to the fact that various groups are under the command of different ministries. Jump training was until recently carried out abroad, mainly in Belgium, and parachute wings are similar to the Belgian insignia, although recently local designs have been seen. During the 1973 war Saudi special forces contingents operated side by side with Syrian forces on the Golan Heights.

There are no detailed reports of operations by Saudi special forces during Operation *Desert Storm*, although some elements could have assisted ground forces during the counter-attacks into Kuwait.

Spain

In line with other NATO members, Spain has committed part of its forces to the Allied Rapid Reaction Corps (ARRC), namely the **Fuerzo de Accion Rapide (FAR)** – Rapid Action Force – which includes the **Brigada Paracaidista (BRIPAC)** – Parachute Brigade. Also committed to NATO is the Spanish Navy's **Unidad Especial de Buceadores de Combate (UEBC)**, which is the equivalent of US SEALs or British SBS.

Spanish marines have been in existence since 1537, when the *Campanias Viejas del Mar de Napole* was formed. Over the centuries, Spain has been one of the world's great seapowers, so her marines have been involved in many battles both at sea and on the land. The modern-day equivalent is the **Tercio de Armada (TEAR)** and it has units based both in the Balearics and the Canary Islands as well as in Spain. TEAR is about the size of a large brigade and is divided into two commands, the first being **Agrupción de Desembarco (AD)** which basically comprises two marine regiments. The second command, **Agrupción de Apoyo de Combate (AAC)** has numerous components such as armour (eighteen M48E medium tanks, seventeen Scorpion CVR(T)s and twenty-seven LVTP 7s which are used to get the marine regiments ashore during an amphibious operation), artillery (two 105 mm towed howitzer batteries and one M109 A2 SP howitzer battery; an anti-tank company of twelve Land Rover-mounted TOWs and eighteen Dragon ATGWs), and a battalion-sized logistic unit of engineer, medical and transport companies.

To support TEAR there is the Naval Group Bravo, which operates a special fleet of ships including two LPAs, three LSTs, one LSD and over thirty large barges. The marines use the same weapons as the Spanish Army so the main assault rifle is the CETME LC and the machine-gun the CETME AMELI whilst the 60 mm and 81 mm LL M86 mortars provide excellent support. Despite being mainly conscripts, who spend just seventeen months with TEAR, the *esprit de corps* is very strong and the units are highly efficient.

Although parachuting was demonstrated in Spain as early as 1935, it was not until the Civil War broke out the following year that both factions began to show any real interest – the Nationalists being trained by the Germans and the Republicans by the Russians. Although both formed small parachute units, none was used in action. The first parachute training school came into existence in 1947 at the Alcantarilla air base (near Murcia) and about a year later the first fully

Spanish marine infantry waiting to board a helicopter. Note the MG3 general-purpose machine-gun, a modernised version of the the classic wartime MG42. (Patrick Allen)

Suitably masked and equipped, a group of Spanish and French SF sit in their helicopter on the way to an operation. (Patrick Allen)

trained paratroopers completed their course. The first parachute battalion was a part of the Spanish Air Force until they gave up their ground troops to the Army, when the **1st Airborne Bandera** was converted into an airborne squadron. It was a highly trained unit capable of all aspects of SF work and composed mainly of free-fall parachutists.

In 1953 it was decided that the squadron should only be made up of legionnaires and mountain troops. The unit saw its first action in the Spanish Sahara in 1956, then again in Morocco up to 1958. By 1965, there were three *Bandera* (Roger de Flor, Roger de Lauria and Ortiz de Zarate), grouped together as the *Brigada Paracaidista* – the Spanish Airborne Brigade. In support of the three parachute battalions there are, as one would expect, artillery, engineer and mixed support battalions. Also within the brigade are specialist HALO companies which act as pathfinders. All members of BRIPAC wear a black beret.

There are still three parachute companies in the Spanish Air Force who wear blue berets and in the Army Ranger-type SF units who wear green berets. These last-named forces are known as **Unidades de Operaciones Especiales (UOE)** and the first company was formed in 1961. The number of companies within the UOE grew considerably until in 1986 it was reorganised. Now it is composed of three types of unit which specialise in certain distinct roles, e.g. anti-terrorism (including hostage recovery), anti-guerrilla warfare and commando-type assignments. They train regularly with similar SF forces in NATO and have a high reputation.

Spanish marine infantry waiting to board their helicopter from the flight deck of one of their amphibious transport vessels (possibly the L51 Galicia). (Patrick Allen)

Spanish SF boarding one of their helicopters (Patrick Allen)

Having made an excellent landing close to another paratrooper this soldier is understandably delighted. (Brigada Paracaidista)

A BRIPAC gun crew load their 105/30 mm light gun, which can fire HE, HESH, Smoke (BE, WP & coloured) and Illuminating rounds at the rate of 6 rpm. (Brigada Paracaidista)

This HMMWV 'Hummer', belonging to the Spanish parachute brigade is equipped with a pedestal-mounted TOW ATGW missile launcher, giving the anti-tank launcher an ideal off-road capability. (Brigada Paracaidista)

The Spanish Legion

It was in 1920 that three battalions *(Banderas)* of the Regiment of Foreigners *(Tercio de Extranjeros)* were first formed after some eight years of lobbying, after it was discovered that the conscript army could not cope with dealing with dissidents in the protectorate of Morocco. They had spent some time studying the French Foreign Legion, however, the main difference to the *Légion étrangère* is that Spanish nationals can join, so the composition has remained at some 90 per cent Spanish and only 10 per cent foreigners. It is true to say that the Regiment was the spearhead of General Franco's Nationalist forces and numbered some eighteen battalions during the Civil War. Postwar it was reduced to six *Banderas* and the Legion posted back to Morocco, where it continued to fight the Moroccan insurgents, until the country became independent, apart from two small Spanish enclaves – Mellila and Ceuta in northern Morocco, where Legion units are still based. There are now some 7,000 men in the Legion which is divided as follows:

1st *Tercio* Gran Capitan (HQ at Mellila) – 1st, 2nd & 3rd *Banderas*

2nd *Tercio* Duque de Alba (HQ at Ceuta) – 4th, 5th & 6th Banderas

3rd *Tercio* Don Juan de Austria (HQ at Fuerteventura, Canary Islands) – 7th & 8th *Banderas* and 1st Light Cavalry Group

4th *Tercio* Alejandro de Farnesio (HQ at Ronda in Malaga) – 9th & 10th *Banderas, Banderas de Operaciones Especiales* (BOEL) – this SF battalion has amphibious, mountaineering, parachuting and LRRP capabilities. It is also the 4th *Tercio* that is assigned to the FAR.

Recruits sign on for a minimum of three years, which can be lengthened to four or five years. Training is intensive, but initially only of three months' duration, so they do not have the time to learn the skills which a modern force really needs, but no doubt this will change as the Legion modernises. Discipline is very strict indeed. To become an officer, legionnaires must first become Spanish citizens. The highest rank that can then be reached by an ex-ranker is major. The parade dress is predominantly green, shirts have short sleeves and open necks and are worn with green breeches and black boots. The green caps have a small red tassel attached, whilst they have white-lined capes with fur collars and hoods. Belts and equipment straps are of webbing rather than the standard leather of the rest of the army.

ABOVE: **Good close-up of two Spanish paratroopers showing their distinctive cap badge.** *(Brigada Paracaidista)*

Spanish SF await the arrival of their helicopter after an operation. *(Patrick Allen)*

Sweden

Founded in 1952, the **Special Forces Corps** of the Swedish Army (FJS) comprises intelligence units operating at military region level, with the main task of gathering information so that higher commanders can make counter-attack decisions should any part of the very long Swedish coastline be invaded by enemy forces. An FJS parachute team consists of five men (the team leader and his deputy are normally second lieutenants, whilst the rest of the team are warrant officers). Like most special forces they have a wide variety of specialities – signal, medic, sniper, demolitions expert, etc. When dropped all are equipped with the basic patrol tent, fieldglasses, short-wave radio, assault or sniper rifle, survival gear, etc. Teams must be prepared to remain active for at least thirty days behind enemy lines.

A hundred volunteers are selected each year, after the normal conscript tests (as undertaken by every young Swede on reaching the age of eighteen), to undergo pre-testing for two days. Training then takes place at Karlsborg, or at their second base, Kiraun, 100 km north of the Arctic Circle, where they go for mountain and winter training. As Sweden has a conscript army, fifteen months is all the training time they have available, starting in June and ending in August the following year. Team leaders are then selected and go on to a further seven months of training. Every second year the teams get three weeks' refresher training. Training comprises three months' basic military training followed by parachute training – static line (twenty jumps) with round canopy and fifteen jumps with square canopy – combat survival, static reconnaissance with the ability to identify all combat vehicles and aircraft that can be expected in the area of operation, sabotage, mainly of railways, and survival after a completed mission by hunting, fishing and using wild plants as food.

In addition to parachute rangers (*Fallskärmjägere)* there are coastal ranger units of attack divers (*Küstjägere*) and the Swedish Air Force Rangers.

Weapons and Equipment

In 1996, the EJS listed their AK5 assault rifle, with its night-sight, and the PSG-90 sniper rifle as two of their main weaponry, however, no doubt they are now also armed with such universal special forces weapons as the Swiss SIG P226 self-loading pistol and the Heckler & Koch MP5 submachine-gun. The world-famous Swedish firm of Bofors has produced the latest edition of its highly effective Carl Gustav M3 84 mm RCL anti-tank weapon for which the HEAT 551C, with its shaped-charge warhead, can penetrate some 400 mm of armour at over 700 m. The other new anti-tank weapon, designed against light armour, is the 20 mm AT-4 CS, which can penetrate nearly 500 mm of homogeneous armour.

Two members of FJS – Swedish Special Forces – prepare to fire an 84 mm Carl Gustav M3 anti-tank weapon which will penetrate armour up to 400 mm thick. (Bofors Carl Gustav AB)

Well camouflaged, this Swedish para ranger, prepares to engage an enemy AFV with his AT-4 CS light armour weapon which will penetrate over 500 mm of armour and weighs just 7.5 kg. (Bofors Carl Gustav AB)

Two Swedish coastal rangers (Küstjägere) carrying a Carl Gustav M3 anti-tank weapon make their way ashore. They are specially trained as attack divers. (Bofors Carl Gustav AB)

Switzerland

The main Swiss special forces unit is the company of Parachute Grenadiers of the Swiss Air Force. Originally known as *Fallschirm-Grenadiers* (Parachute Grenadiers) they are now called *Fernspah-Grenadiers* (Long-Range Reconnaissance Grenadiers), the name change coming in 1980, when they were given the new role of long-range reconnaissance patrolling (LRRP). The company, usually just called FSK 17, has been in existence since the early 1970s, as has the training school where such techniques as static-line and free-fall parachuting are taught, as are LRRP, gathering intelligence, demolitions, survival skills and pistol markmanship (most important as the FSK 17 are sometimes armed with just their pistols, knives and grenades).

There are usually about 500–700 applicants each year out of which 300 are selected. These undergo a thorough medical examination at the Swiss Air Force Medical Centre, which further reduces the number to about eighty who are fit for the tough training that will follow. The volunteers are still only eighteen years old when they commence their first two-week basic parachuting course which includes ten static-line and twenty-five free-fall descents, combined with all the necessary theoretical studies. After that there are only some forty left and they return for a further two-week advanced training. This course includes a total of thirty-five free-fall descents. Only about thirty eventually qualify and pass on to yet more medical and psychological examinations before being permitted to enter the *Fernspahe Schule*.

At this stage there are just twenty left, and they carry out twenty weeks of basic training, which is divided into three main periods – five weeks' infantry training, ten weeks' reconnaissance techniques and five weeks' military free-fall parachuting. It is a tough course, with the recruits constantly being put under more and more pressure. Combat survival training takes place in an inhospitable rocky area of deep ravines and high cliffs near the Swiss/Italian border, where they spend a week practising their survival skills. Parachute training is equally rigorous, with jumps being made with weapons and equipment, from varying altitudes and in all weathers. The high standard they reach can be judged by the fact that they won the International Military Competition in 1981, just one year after they had changed to the LRRP role, and since that date have never been out of the top three places!

FSK 17 comprises about 100 all ranks, divided into three sub-units of equal size. As with the majority of SF units the basic patrol size is four men, and FSK 17 has pioneered the 'tactical diamond' technique whereby all four exit from the aircraft at the same time and hold onto each other in free-fall, only breaking apart to deploy their canopies. This means that they land within yards of one another, which is ideal when dropping in poor visibility, or at night or when the DZ is small. In addition to HALO and HAHO drops, they also practise dropping from as low as 100 m using the American T10 non-steerable military parachute instead of their normal MT-IXX

Equipment

They must be skilled in the use of all types of personal and infantry weapons, especially assault rifles and the like. They normally wear standard-pattern Swiss camouflage clothing, but with fibre jump helmets and jumpboots. On their shoulders they wear the company shoulder title '17'.

Combat Swimmers

Up to the early 1980s, each of the field corps in the Swiss Army had a platoon of combat swimmers, trained in SCUBA and underwater demolition techniques, for use in the larger lakes such as Geneva and Constance. They were supposedly disbanded in 1980, but no doubt some will remain, working with the light gunboats which are employed on the lakes for security purposes.

Landings may well be into water as Switzerland has large lakes – hence the frogman's gear on this FSK 17 paratrooper. (armeefotodienst BERN)

Free-falling onto the roof of the world! This spectacular photograph of four FSK 17 free-fallers gives a clear indication of the expertise that has kept them at the forefront of competitive military parachuting for many years. (armeefotodienst BERN)

Then it is off into the forest, carrying everything on one's back and overcoming any obstacle in your path, like this rushing mountain stream. Their weapons are the Swiss-made SG550 or Stgw 90 assault rifle, designed by the Swiss SIG company and replacing the earlier SIG 510 series. (armeefotodienst BERN)

Syria

The Syrian armed forces have perhaps the most powerful and combat-experienced commando units in the Arab world today. The special forces, also known as the **Al-Wahdat al-Khassa** (Special Units) are regarded as elite, their men carefully selected from volunteers for their physical fitness and total loyalty to the regime. They are given the best and most modern weapon systems and equipment available.

Although figures vary somewhat, the best assessment seems to indicate that there is one special forces division (the **14th Special Forces Division**) based in Lebanon with its four SF regiments: the **55th, 54th, 46th** and **35th**, all based in the Beirut area. There are also the **44th Special Forces Regiment** near Chikka, the **53rd** south of Haiba near Tripoli and the **804th** and **41st** east of Juniya.

A commando regiment is composed of three companies (para-trained) and supported by a 82 mm mortar company, a machine-gun platoon and an anti-tank company. Other special forces units include one rapid-deployment brigade (airborne) and the **Saraya al Difa** (Defence Companies) formerly under the command of Rifaat Assad, the president's brother. The battalion-sized force may have been reorganised since, but it should include two paratroop forces of battalion size.

The Syrian special forces have their origin with the first parachute company raised in 1958. Their first combat experience was in 1973 when 82nd Commando Battalion trained and carried out a superbly executed attack on the IDF monitoring station on top of Mount Hermon, at the start of the Yom Kippur War. Three years later, commando units fought against the PLO in Lebanon and gained considerable experience in urban warfare in the coastal towns. During the 1982 Lebanon War, no fewer than ten commando battalions fought against the Israelis on all fronts. One particular successful action was fought by a Syrian commando battalion against an IDF armoured unit at Sultan Yakoub, in which they inflicted heavy casualties in a well-laid ambush.

← Commandos

← Frontier Guards

↓ Paratroops

Equipment and Uniform
The insignia is composed of a skull and crossed-scimitars. Lizard-pattern camouflage uniforms and bright red or orange berets are worn. Uniforms vary in pattern from one unit to another, thus different camouflage fatigues can be seen, indicating the different status of the unit. In Lebanon, Syrian commando soldiers were seen wearing Pakistani camouflage suits. Combat headwear includes Soviet parachute helmets covered with camouflage cloth. Standard fatigue cloth caps are worn off duty or in non-combat activities. US Army field jackets are also worn during winter. Lately, new camouflage suits have been sighted in Lebanon, not the reddish-coloured lizard pattern, but sand-coloured fatigues. Body armour and riot control equipment, is also worn in urban areas.

Individual weapons include the TT-33 Tokarev 9 mm Makarov, the M23/M25 SMG and SSG69 sniper assault rifles and the AK-47 and AKM Kalashnikov assault rifles.

Taiwan

Like mainland China's special forces, Taiwanese SF have their origins in the US parachute-trained units formed at the end of the Second World War, some of which stayed behind while others fled with the Nationalists to Taiwan. By 1958 the **1st Special Forces Group** had been formed and in the following years another three groups were raised. By the mid-1990s these units were:

- 1st Peace Preservation Police Corps Special Weapons and Tactics Unit
- Military Police Special Service Company (approximate strength 100 men, divided into three platoons; training includes parachute and ranger techniques as well as martial arts, and lasts for nine months)
- Airborne and Special Warfare Command Special Operations Unit (strength 100; training shared with US at Fort Bragg and US Ranger School)
- Chinese Marine Corps Special Operations Unit (strength 100 men, responsible for maritime security; SCUBA and airborne qualified)

All units are under the control of Security Task Force Headquarters, which is directly answerable to the Prime Minister.

With increasing demilitarisation and democracy internal CT duties have been allocated to the regional National Police SWAT teams rather than their military counterparts.

Armed with a Type 65 assault rifle – a local copy of the US M16 – soldiers of the Taiwanese Special Forces on jungle patrol stop for a radio check. (MPL International Ltd)

Turkey

Given its strategically central position sharing borders with many countries, linking Asia and Europe, the Black Sea and the Mediterranean, it is no surprise that Turkey possesses armed forces of close to a million men, including substantial special forces. There are three airborne brigades and at least one counter-terrorist special forces battalion of approximately 150 men, with similar capabilities and training methods to the British SAS and US Delta Force. Turkey's membership of NATO means it also shares much of the Western weaponry and equipment used by those formations.

In 1949 the USA began paratroop training and supplying Turkish forces, with officers and men also being sent to the USA. These were then integrated into the **1st Airborne Platoon of the Guards Regiment**. In 1958 the **2nd Airborne Platoon** was formed, and by 1963 a third had also come into existence, making a three-battalion airborne brigade. These units saw action when they were dropped on Cyprus in 1974, where they soon defeated their Greek foes. Following this success a further two brigades were created to cover a wider spectrum of missions, one airborne, one para commando and one para-marine.

Each brigade comprises 5,000 men, distributed among three battalions and support companies, and the airborne brigade possesses its own artillery company.

Having a long coastline, Turkey also places great emphasis on naval elements. There are thus three naval commando brigades:

- **1st Commando Brigade**, specialising in *su alti savunma* (SAS) or underwater defence; SAS is based in Kayseri. They have recently been deployed to various areas in south-east Anatolia against separatists and during the ensuing operations the brigade earned itself the highest award of the Turkish Armed Forces, the Distinguished Courage Medal.
- **2nd Commando Brigade**, specialising in *su alti taaruz* (SAT) or underwater attack; SAT is based at Bolu. It also was deployed to south-east Anatolia to fight Kurdish separatists, where it also won the country's highest honours for its efforts.
- **3rd Commando Brigade**, specialising in conventional amphibious operations, including infiltration from the sea, long-range reconnaissance and intelligence gathering, and sabotage. It has bases at Foca and Izmir.

United Kingdom

The **5th Airborne Brigade** was formed in 1983, when the 5th Infantry Brigade, which had been deployed in the highly successful capture of the Falkland Islands in 1981, was enlarged and redesignated. The **24th Airmobile Brigade** was formed in 1988, when the 24th Infantry Brigade, was redesignated and later assigned (in 1993) to the Multinational Division (Central) (MND(C)) as part of the Allied Rapid Reaction Corps (ARRC).

Formed in 2000 to replace these units, **16 Air Assault Brigade** has a strength of nearly 10,000 personnel and is capable of striking quickly and deeply into enemy territory, enabling the British Army to react even more rapidly than ever before. The new brigade makes use of a wide range of modern equipment from the latest Apache helicopter to airmobile artillery and air defence missiles. Over the next three years the new brigade will pull together all its various elements and by 2004 will be fully capable in the air manoeuvre role, when the last Aviation Regiment is combat ready.

Air assault operations are generally very complex and require effective command and control and robust communications. 16 Air Assault Brigade's **HQ and Signal Squadron** has a number of configurations, from a manpack tactical HQ to a fully equipped main HQ. It also has a joint (Army/RAF) HQ based in Colchester, to provide the direction and co-ordination required for air assault operations. The parachute-deployable 216 Signal Squadron is responsible for establishing and maintaining communications networks and systems to the fighting units and rearwards to its Forward Mounting Base (FMB). It also provides the infrastructure for all levels of Brigade HQ in the field.

The **Pathfinder Platoon** is 16 Air Assault Brigade's advance force and its organic reconnaissance force. Such operations will include covert reconnaissance, location and marking of drop zones, tactical landing zones and helicopter landing zones for subsequent air assault operations. Once the main force has landed, the platoon provides tactical intelligence vital to the operational decision-making Brigade HQ.

The **3rd and 4th Regiments, Army Air Corps (AAC)** based at Wattisham, and the **9th Regiment, AAC** based at Dishforth are the Brigade's aviation regiments. Each has two anti-tank squadrons, a light battlefield helicopter (LBH) squadron and an aviation workshop. Anti-tank squadrons currently provide the combat power with the Lynx Mk 7 equipped with the TOW missile system, working alongside Gazelle helicopters which provide the reconnaissance capability. The LBH squadrons are equipped with Lynx Mk 9 LBHs. The role of the LBH is to move small groups of soldiers around the brigade area (e.g. infantry, Javelin air defence teams, and engineers). The REME-manned aviation workshop provides first line helicopter maintenance support. In 1996, a contract was signed for sixty-seven Apache Longbow Attack helicopters for the British Army with an inservice date of December 2005. Present plans are for the Brigade to have 48 Apaches (each regiment has two squadrons of eight Apaches), plus a squadron of Lynx providing the intimate support.

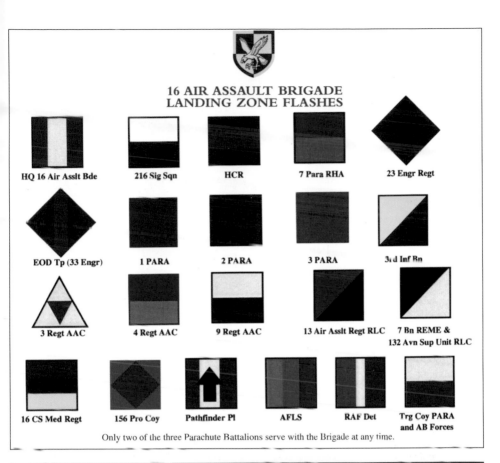

16 AIR ASSAULT BRIGADE LANDING ZONE FLASHES

HQ 16 Air Asslt Bde	216 Sig Sqn	HCR	7 Para RHA	23 Engr Regt
EOD Tp (33 Engr)	1 PARA	2 PARA	3 PARA	3rd Inf Bn
3 Regt AAC	4 Regt AAC	9 Regt AAC	13 Air Asslt Regt RLC	7 Bn REME & 132 Avn Sup Unit RLC
16 CS Med Regt	156 Pro Coy	Pathfinder Pl	AFLS	RAF Det	Trg Coy PARA and AB Forces

Only two of the three Parachute Battalions serve with the Brigade at any time.

Widely used by SF is the Land Rover Defender Multi Role Combat Vehicle (MRCV), which can carry a mix of weapons, such as a 30 mm cannon and 7.62 mm GPMG as seen here, plus an 81 mm mortar and LAW 80. (Land Rover)

Men of 16 Air Assault Brigade firing an 81 mm mortar during Ex Monoprix in Northern Kenya. The L16 mortar is in service with all British Army infantry battalions and has a maximum range of 5,560 m. (Crown Copyright)

The main ground fighting elements of the Brigade are found from the three **air assault infantry battalions**, two of which are always provided from the Parachute Regiment (specialising in paratroop assault operations) and one from Line Infantry (specialising in TALO and rapid air land operations). All air assault infantry battalions are practised in the conduct of massed support helicopter operations by day and night. Each infantry battalion has a five-company structure – three rifle companies, a support company and an HQ company. Each battalion has nine 81 mm mortars, eighty GPMGs, fourteen .50 cal Browning Heavy MGs and sixteen MILAN anti-tank missile systems.

The **7th Para, RHA**, directly supports the Brigade with three paratroop batteries of 105 mm light guns. Each battery has six guns, which have a range of 17 km and fire a shell every 10 seconds. Their fire is directed by the regiment's forward observation officers (FOOs), who normally deploy forward with infantry companies.

The **21st Defence Battery, RA**, based in Thorney Island is equipped with the Javelin, which is shoulder launched singly or from a mobile launcher holding three missiles. This provides for highly manoeuvrable and lethal close air defence out to 5,500 m.

The **9th Parachute Squadron, RE**, based in Aldershot and 51 Field Squadron, RE, based in Ripon, provide engineering support, their main tasks being to ensure that friendly forces can move freely on the battlefield whilst denying the enemy freedom of movement. The Brigade can also call upon a squadron of the **Household Cavalry Regiment (HCR)**

Two Rangers of the 1st Battalion The Royal Irish Rangers, one armed with the SA80 5.56 mm Individual Weapon (IW), the other with the 5.56 mm Light Support Weapon (LSW). There were problems with both these weapons when they entered service, however they have now been rectified. Note the good close-up of the 16 Air Assault Brigade flash. (Crown Copyright)

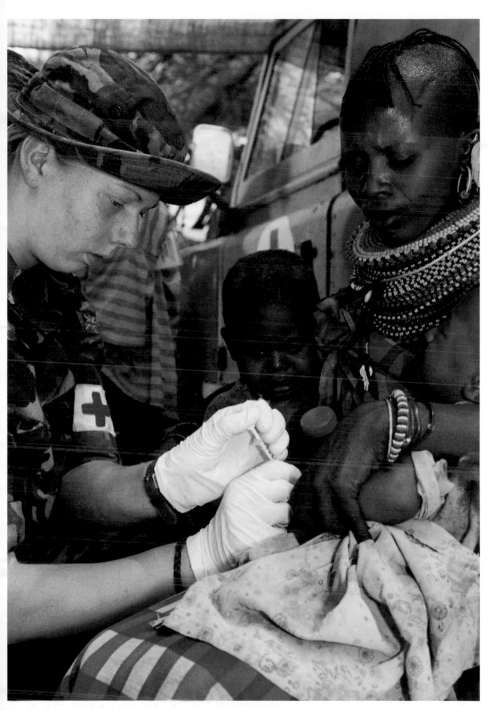

'Hearts & Minds' forms a vital part of soldiering these days. Here a medical orderly of 16 Close Support Medical Regiment administers to a tiny patient in Kenya, 1999. *(Crown Copyright)*

belonging to 3 (UK) Division, to provide medium reconnaissance as and when required. It has three troops each of four Scimitar reconnaissance vehicles, equipped with Rarden cannon and co-axial GPMGs.

The **RAF Support Helicopter Force** provides helicopters for mobility, normally eighteen Chinooks and eighteen Pumas. On exercises and deployment these helicopters are controlled by Support Helicopter Force HQ, which is normally located with Brigade HQ. The Brigade is also supported by the largest air transport fleet in Western Europe, comprising fifty-five Hercules C-130 aircraft, which are used for parachute, TALO and rapid air land deployments. The Brigade is the largest recipient of air despatch support. Combat supplies, including light armour and guns are delivered to **47 Air Despatch Squadron**, where they are arranged into manageable loads and packed into containers or onto platforms. Parachutes are then fitted and loads installed into the aircraft, before being despatched to units on the ground.

The Parachute Regiment

Integral infantry components at the heart of the new 16 Air Assault Brigade are the three parachute battalions of the Parachute Regiment, 1, 2 & 3

Paratroop Battalions, two of which are always part of the Brigade air assault infantry. Unlike the Italians, the Russians and the Germans all of whom had appreciated the potential of the paratrooper well before the Second World War began, Britain was slow to organise either paratroop or gliderborne forces, so it was not until late 1940 that Prime Minister Winston Churchill managed to force the War Office to form the first airborne unit (made up of volunteers from 2 Commando). Thereafter volunteers came forward rapidly and in considerable numbers, the **2nd Airborne Brigade** being formed in 1942. They fought in Tunisia (but were not airdropped), soon earning from the Germans the nickname *Die Roten Teufel* (The Red Devils). Later, in 1943, now enlarged as the **1st Airborne Division**, they dropped in Sicily, wearing their famous 'Pegasus' airborne patch. They went on to win imperishable glory whilst holding 'a bridge too far' at Arnhem in September 1944, whilst the 6th Airborne Division, which had been formed in the UK prior to D-Day, spearheaded the Normandy invasion in June 1944.

After the war, the Paras, who had been awarded three Victoria Crosses, were affected by the inevitable cuts and 'reorganisations' that plague armies in

This paratrooper is operating a RACAL Panther P handheld radio, with Cobra modular radio ancillaries. He wears the famous red beret and winged parachute badge. (Michael Blackburn Photography for RACAL)

peacetime. However, throughout the immediate postwar era and after, they were always in the forefront of the internal security operations which went along with Britain's withdrawal from the Empire. They fought in all the major troublespots such as Palestine, Malaya, Suez, Aden and Borneo, then in the Falklands.

After the Falklands conflict, yet more reorganisations took place, whilst the Paras took their turn in dealing with the troubles in Northern Ireland and elsewhere. In 1982, the 5th Infantry Brigade became the **5th Airborne Brigade**, then in the June 1998, another major defence review saw the formation of **24 Airmobile Brigade**. Now they have once again been at the centre of a major reorganisation which has seen them move from Aldershot to Colchester, whilst the new 16 Air Assault Brigade of which they are a vital part has come into existence.

All officers and men are volunteers and have to attend a rigorous two-day preselection course at the Parachute Regimental Depot. This is followed by an extremely tough recruit training course lasting some twenty-three weeks. The first eight weeks are spent on general military training as undertaken by every recruit who joins the British Army (drill, weapon training, fieldcraft, etc.) Next follows a period of external leadership training – canoeing, rock climbing and abseiling – then a period on infantry team skills, including weapon training on basic infantry personal weapons. Then they attend the parachute selection course – the 'P' Company (the Pre-Parachute Selection Company) week – after which those selected will go on to further training. By the end of their tough training course, which is not dissimilar to that undertaken by the Royal Marine Commando recruits, only some 35 per cent of those who started will have stayed the distance and earned their wings at a special passing-out parade held to mark the culmination of their recruit training. However, training is never finished and, when not on operations, paratroopers spend much of their time learning new skills and honing old ones.

A Royal Marine Commando aiming a LAW 80 shoulder launched anti-tank missile system, which fires a 10 lb 94 mm HEAT rocket. (Hunting Engineering)

Equipment

Paratroops are equipped with standard British Army weapons and equipment, being trained in the wide variety of skills required by the modern-day infantryman (e.g. signals, assault pioneer, support weapons, sniping, etc.); indeed all take the fullest advantage of new weaponry and equipment entering service, the rigorous life of the paratrooper being an ideal way of fully testing new kit.

The only feature that distinguishes the Paras from other soldiers is their red beret which can only be worn by members of the Parachute Regiment with their equally distinctive cap badge, or by those members of other corps and units who are parachute trained, and then *only* when they are serving with a parachute unit.

The Royal Marines

Although the Royal Marines (RM) are – and always have been – an integral part of the Royal Navy, with detachments serving afloat on at least a dozen ships, they are trained and equipped primarily for land warfare. Since their creation in 1942, Royal Marine Commandos have engaged on active operations across the globe. The Royal Marines currently number some 500 officers and 5,500 men, ready to be deployed on operations anywhere in the world. The bulk of this manpower is grouped into lightly armed battalion-sized units, known as commandos. Currently there are three commandos and together they form **3 Commando Brigade**. The Brigade's unique capabilities and deployability were again recognised in 1996 when it became one of the core brigades within the Joint Rapid Deployment Force (JRDF). As part of the JRDF it retains a lead commando group ready to deploy worldwide at very short notice.

Up to the Second World War every ship of cruiser size and above had an RM detachment fully integrated into the ship's company, but able to be deployed as a landing party when required. In 1937, it was proposed to employ RM as specialised amphibious troops and that was the start of the change to commandos. During the war RM Commandos carried out raiding activities on the French, Belgian and Dutch coasts. During the D-Day invasion 47 and 48 RM Commandos went ashore with the first wave and suffered heavy casualties. Since the end of the war, there have been few years when the Marines have not been on active service.

In the 1998 Strategic Defence Review (SDR) it was agreed that 3 Commando Brigade would be retained in full and that the modernisation programme would continue. The helicopter carrier HMS *Ocean* (known as a Landing Platform Helicopter), which was recently

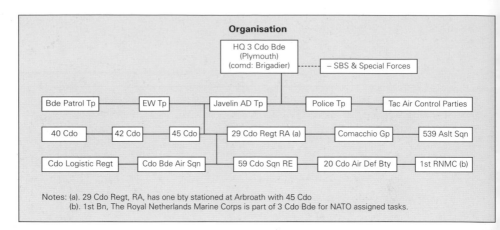

Organisation

```
                        HQ 3 Cdo Bde
                          (Plymouth)
                      (comd: Brigadier) ------- – SBS & Special Forces
```

Bde Patrol Tp	EW Tp	Javelin AD Tp	Police Tp	Tac Air Control Parties
40 Cdo	42 Cdo	45 Cdo	29 Cdo Regt RA (a)	Comacchio Gp	539 Aslt Sqn
Cdo Logistic Regt	Cdo Bde Air Sqn	59 Cdo Sqn RE	20 Cdo Air Def Bty	1st RNMC (b)

Notes: (a). 29 Cdo Regt, RA, has one bty stationed at Arbroath with 45 Cdo
(b). 1st Bn, The Royal Netherlands Marine Corps is part of 3 Cdo Bde for NATO assigned tasks.

launched and is currently on its sea trials, can carry twelve Sea King HAS 4 troop lift helicopters and six Lynx HAS 8 attack helicopters (these could be replaced by EH-101 and Apaches by the end of the decade). It has a crew of 250 all ranks and is capable of taking an entire marine commando of up to 850 men. There are also plans to procure two landing ships logistic (LSL) and two new landing platform docks (LPD), the latter to replace the current assault vessels HMS *Fearless* (launched 1965) and HMS *Intrepid* (launched 1967), both of which proved their worth in the Falklands conflict but are now getting too old.

Orders have been placed with VSEL for the two new vessels to be named HMS *Albion* and HMS

Royal Marines Uniform

Royal Marine Commandos wear the distinctive green beret with the globe and laurel badge, but in general terms their combat uniforms, weapons and equipment is the same as those of the British Army. As the organisational table explains, the artillery, air, engineer, logistic, etc. support is provided from units seconded by the British Army, who wear their own regimental insignia with the commandos' green beret.

SBS personnel wear standard RM uniform, with RM parachutist wings (on the right shoulder) and the Swimmer Canoeist badge on the right forearm (the latter is not worn by officers).

Spray soaks a Royal Marine Commando of the Comacchio Group, RM during a highspeed chase on Loch Fyne. (MPL International Ltd)

*Seen here in the lower of the two docks is the first of the two new Landing Platform Docks that will replace the existing HMS **Fearless** and* Intrepid. *It will have 17,000 tonnes displacement, be 171 m long and have a crew of 325.* (BAE Systems Marine)

Bulwark, which were due to enter service in 2001 and 2003 but have been delayed. Both will be 171 m long, displacing 15,000 tons, and their diesel engines will give them a top speed of 18 knots. There will be two flight deck spaces for FH-101 helicopters, four LCU landing craft will be carried in the well deck, with another five landing craft in davits. The crew will number some 325 and 650 embarked troops can be carried.

There are also specialist units, the main one of which is the **Special Boat Service (SBS)**, the naval equivalent of the Army's Special Air Service. It used to be called the Special Boat Squadron, but was renamed in the early 1990s. It may be assigned to the Commando Brigade to conduct advance force operations. Like the SAS, its personnel are divided into four-man, normally lightly equipped, patrols. Its origins go back to the specialised units raised during the Second World War for raiding and reconnaissance of enemy-held coastlines. Since the war they have been used on numerous occasions, for example in the Oman and Borneo and during the Falklands War in

1982, when they were involved in the recapture of South Georgia.

Personnel are all volunteers from within the Royal Marines with at least two years' service, and, as can be imagined, competition for the few entries that occur each year is fierce, with only a small number of applicants qualifying at the end of a gruelling three-week entry/selection course. Those who pass then undertake an equally arduous fifteen-week training course in demolitions and advanced weapon handling, using such weapons as the silenced version of the H&K MP5 submachine-gun and other weapons as used by the SAS, diving using closed circuit aqualungs, reconnaissance work, seamanship and navigation, and the use of small amphibious craft such as the specially-produced Klepper Mk 13 collapsible canoe and the larger Gemini which is powered by a 40 hp outboard. Finally they must pass a four-week parachute course before joining an operational unit.

The SBS specialises in mounting clandestine operations against targets located at sea, along enemy coastlines and in rivers and harbours. The personnel are highly trained swimmers/canoeists/parachutists and are undoubtedly one of the best-trained units among this type of special forces.

The other specialised unit, known as **Comacchio Group**, was formed in 1980 and has the task of guarding UK oil-rigs and associated installations from a variety of threats, including terrorist attacks.

A RN clearance diver surfaces after carrying out a beach reconnaissance in Loch Fyne. He is attached to the Comacchio Group, RM who are responsible for anti-terrorist duties in connection with maintaining the security of Britain's nuclear deterrent. (MPL International Ltd)

The Special Air Service (SAS)

The **SAS** is one of the most highly trained special forces units in the world. Its reputation and abilities are legendary and its 'Who dares wins' motto, winged dagger beret badge and all-black anti-terrorist clothing have become almost mystical symbols in today's fight against all forms of international terrorism. This tends to give the SAS an aura of invincibility out of all proportion to its current size, which basically comprises just one regular (**22 SAS**) and two TA (**21 SAS (Artists' Rifles)** and **23 SAS**) regiments, with attached squadrons (264 (SAS) Signal Squadron, a regular signal squadron with 22 SAS and 63 (SAS) Signal Squadron TA with the two TA regiments).

One of the major roles of the SAS is covert intelligence gathering which by its very nature must be clandestine, so overexposure is not welcomed, despite the very considerable public interest which at times almost reaches fever pitch – for example, when black-clothed SAS men were photographed in May 1980, on the balcony of the Iranian Embassy in London during their highly successful hostage-rescue operation.

The SAS is the only regiment in the British Army which does not recruit directly from the general public and its standards are so high that only a very small proportion of those who volunteer from within the Army are initially accepted, and an even smaller percentage go on to pass the exhaustive selection and training courses.

The SAS was evolved from a handful of unconventional soldiers under Colonel David Stirling who operated very successfully behind enemy lines in North Africa in 1941. The first unit to be formed was called L Detachment, Special Air Service Brigade, the 1st Special Air Service Brigade being the name of a bogus formation which was part of a plan to persuade the enemy that there was a complete British parachute and glider brigade in the Middle East at that time. Its operations can be summarised in Stirling's own words as: 'firstly, raids in depth behind enemy lines, attacking HQ nerve centres, landing grounds, supply lines and so on; and secondly, the mounting of sustained strategic activity from secret bases within hostile territory and, if the opportunity existed, recruiting, training, arming and co-ordinating local guerrilla elements'. Operations in the Central Mediterranean led on to the formation in the UK of a major force for operations in north-west Europe, which by January 1944 had grown into an SAS Brigade, which comprised two British regiments (1 and 2 SAS), two French regiments (3 and 4 SAS), a Belgian squadron (later 5 SAS), together with the vitally necessary signal squadrons.

Immediately after the war, 'private armies' like the SAS, went out of fashion, but it was soon recognised that there was a continuing requirement for a

This soldier is dressed in black Nomex overalls and hood as worn by SAS Counter Revolutionary personnel. He is firing a 9 mm Browning L1A1 pistol, whilst abseiling down a rope. He also wears an S10 respirator and carries a 'flash-bang' stun grenade (MPL International Ltd)

clandestine force to carry out covert operations during the withdrawal from Empire. The SAS was officially reborn in 1950, when a TA unit, the Artists' Rifles, was converted into the **21st Special Air Service Regiment (Artists' Rifles) Volunteers**. In 1952, the Malayan Scouts (SAS), which had been built up during the Malayan emergency, was redesignated as the **22nd Special Air Service Regiment**, thus returning the SAS to regular service in the British Army order of battle. Operations in Aden, the Persian Gulf, Kenya, Borneo, Oman and of course Northern Ireland occupied most of their time, as the SAS gradually enlarged its roles to encompass counter-terrorists as well as those of anti-guerrilla and internal security operations. Small SAS elements have also been involved in working with the special forces of foreign countries, such as the operation to retake a West German airliner in Mogadishu in 1977, when they worked in co-operation with a GSG9 unit. Probably the most public display of their considerable skills was the six-day siege of the Iranian Embassy, which was ended spectacularly by the SAS on 5 May 1980. The hostages were rescued, four of the five terrorists were killed and the SAS, who had sustained no casualties, received far more publicity than they ever wanted.

Highly successful SAS operations in the Falklands War followed, showing that they were still capable of carrying out more conventional but still covert military tasks, whilst in the Gulf War of 1991, SAS teams were inserted into Iraq, their prime targets being Saddam Hussein's Scud missile launchers and signal communication centres. This type of task has continued during the UN/NATO operations in Bosnia, where they have operated behind Serbian lines providing intelligence and calling down airstrikes on suitable targets, such as armour and artillery positions. Clearly the SAS of today still practise and improve those skills for which they were originally established, despite the more popular public image of their activities in the forefront of counter-terrorist operations.

Much has been written about the SAS, both fact and fiction, however, as their official historian, John Strawson, succinctly put it, 'It is clear that no service either to them or to the nation can be done by recounting their recent activities in a number of countries, including our own.'

Control of the three SAS regiments and their associated units is exercised by the Director, Special Forces. All three work closely together, with strong regular cadres in each TA regiment. Each is some 600–700 all ranks in strength and divided into four squadrons. Within the squadron are four sixteen-man troops, who normally work on operations as four-man patrols. Clearly in order to function they must have the necessary administrative support as and when required, including all forms of transport as necessary, so that they can move by sea, land and air.

They hold selection testing twice a year, winter and summer, and can initially have up to 180 candidates, all of whom are regular Army volunteers. However, by the end of the selection and training phases only about eight to ten will finish the course and be selected. Initially the first phase (four weeks) is to discover whether they have the physical and mental stamina to deal with any operational situation in any terrain from the Arctic to the jungle, which may well begin by being dropped into enemy territory by parachute, using special parachutes that may be HAHO or HALO, or by sea using a canoe or inflatable, or by land either on foot or in a vehicle. They must also be versed in other skills such as patrolling, demolitions, signals, medical and hostage operations, but these are covered in later phases. The initial phase consists of gruelling physical tests, based on a series of cross-country route marches (taps) in the Brecon Beacons, carrying heavy loads (over 60 lb) between a series of checkpoints. By the end of this period they must be able to walk four miles in under thirty minutes and swim two in ninety minutes. Only some 10 per cent survive to pass the fitness phase. This is followed by two four-week periods of weapons and jungle training. In the first of these all types of weapons are used from pistols and rifles to machine-guns and other support weapons. Also included are foreign weapons like the AK-47 Kalashnikov. Despite this weapons efficiency SAS troopers are taught to capture rather than to kill, but if they are forced to do the latter they must do so quickly and efficiently.

The next phase is jungle training – a month in a rain forest, where, after three weeks' training the culmination is a week-long exercise, testing all the skills they have learnt such as jungle navigation, living in the jungle, jungle first aid, etc. In addition to these three main phases there are other shorter training periods on general field medicine and trauma management, signals, artillery spotting, demolitions and sabotage, sniping and, for some, language training. The final part of the training and selection is an escape and evasion phase where would-be SAS troopers must take part in a five-day escape and evasion exercise, being hunted by other troops in a hostile environment, then facing interrogation at the hands of experts.

The Gurkhas

The two regular battalions of the **Royal Gurkha Rifles (RGR)**, together with their supporting engineers, signals and transport, make up the Brigade of Gurkhas, an important part of the British Army 'fire brigade', being used whenever there is a trouble spot where well-trained, highly professional troops are needed in a hurry – witness their recent use in East Timor.

The men of the hill tribes of Nepal have long been famed for their martial prowess and after the inconclusive Anglo-Nepal War (1814–16), a Treaty of Friendship was signed which allowed Gurkhas to enlist voluntarily in the armies of the honourable East India Company. The Gurkha regiments were absorbed into the British Army in 1858, then in 1947, when India achieved its independence, six of the ten Gurkha regiments became part of the new Indian Army, whilst the remaining four (**2nd, 6th, 7th and 10th Gurkha Rifles**) along with the other units, were incorporated into the British Army. Over the years the Gurkhas have been subject to cuts in line with the rest of the British Army, but have managed to retain their individuality, pride and fighting spirit.

Gurkhas distinguished themselves in both world wars, first against the Turks in Gallipoli and Mesopotamia, when they were awarded two Victoria Crosses; then against the Germans and Italians in Tunisia and Italy and the Japanese in Burma, when they won a staggering ten more. Since the war they have shown their considerable skills in jungle fighting, first in Malaya, then Borneo. They also played a major part in the successful liberation of the Falklands, landing at San Carlos Bay and taking part in the final assault on Port Stanley. They have served in Northern Ireland and were seen in East Timor, two platoons providing support for 1 Para battlegroup when it was deployed to assist UN troops in Sierra Leone.

Would-be recruits – and there are many thousands of them as every young male Gurkha wants to be a soldier – are signed up at the age of seventeen, in Nepal by itinerant ex-Gurkha regular soldiers (known as 'gallah-wallahs'), who receive a bounty for each successful signing. The minimum term of service is fifteen years and they first undergo an extensive nine-month course, which usually begins each January in the UK. The course has to be long as many recruits are from faraway mountain villages, with few modern amenities and not much schooling. However, the majority quickly settle down and become magnificent soldiers. Since the closure of the Training Depot of the Brigade of Gurkhas in Hong Kong, Gurkha recruits have been trained in the UK.

Modern Gurkha units have few British officers below the CO, the majority now being Gurkhas who have come up through the ranks and have vast experience of soldiering. The most senior of these, known as the Gurkha Major, acts as adviser to the CO on all Gurkha matters.

Risking leeches and other underwater hazards, this Gurkha soldier wades up a jungle river in Belize on a routine patrol looking for insurgents crossing from Guatemala. (MPL International Ltd)

United States of America

Special Operations Forces (SOF) have been a part of US military history since the colonial era. In every conflict since the Revolutionary War, the USA has employed special operations tactics and strategies to exploit an enemy's vulnerability. These operations have always been carried out by specially trained people with a remarkable inventory of skills.

USSOCOM Insignia
The distinctive USSOCOM insignia is an adaptation of one originally designed by the first and only director of the Office of Strategic Services, Major-General William 'Wild Bill' Donavan, during the Second World War. The background colour is black showing that special operations activities take place mostly under the cover of darkness; the spearhead symbolises 'attack' – how SOF lead the way to subdue enemy defences; the three golden rings around the shaft of the spear indicate that forces are assigned from the Army, Air Force and Navy; the four stars represent the four compass points, emphasising a global mission; the braided cord around the shield symbolises strength through unity.

Although the Office of Strategic Services (OSS) co-ordinated 'unconventional warfare' during the Second World War, and the 10th Special Forces Group was resuscitated in the early 1950s, it was not until the late 1950s and early 1960s, when the USA started to get more and more heavily involved in the war between North and South Vietnam, that SOF began to operate in significant numbers. President Kennedy had an abiding interest in SOF, and in 1961 authorised the wearing of the Green Beret, which was to become such an emotive symbol. It was ten more years before the last 'Green Beret' left Vietnam, whilst they continued to operate in other parts of the world, giving advice and specialised training to friendly armies.

UNITED STATES SPECIAL OPERATIONS COMMAND BADGES
Centre – USSOCOM
Top left – US Army Special Operations Command (USASOC)
Top right – Naval Special Warfare Command (NAVSPECWARCOM)
Bottom left – Air Force Special Operations Command (AFSOC)
Bottom right – Joint Special Operations Command (JSOC)

However, back in the USA, there was an undercurrent of distrust and suspicion within the rest of the armed forces as to the need for such elite forces, whose standards of efficiency and capability were undoubtedly declining.

The disastrous failure of Operation *Eagle Claw*, mounted to rescue fifty-three American hostages from

The Mark V Special Operations Craft (SOC) is ideal for use in medium range, bad weather infiltration/extraction of SOF or for limited coastal patrols and interdiction. It has a range of over 600 nm and a sustained top speed in excess of 40 knots. (USSOCOM)

background of the downsizing of the US military due to the demise of the Soviet Union. However, at the same time, the appearance of new aggressor states, heightened regional instabilities and the proliferation of weapons of mass destruction all led to an increased need for SOF.

USSOCOM comprises some 46,000 Army, Navy and Air Force SOF personnel, both active and reserve, organised into a variety of land, sea and aerospace forces which include:

- US Army special forces, **75th Ranger Regiment, 160th Special Operations Aviation Regiment (Airborne)**, and psychological and civil affairs units
- US Navy **sea-air-land forces** (SEALs), special boat units and SEAL delivery units
- US Air Force **special operations squadrons** (fixed and rotary wing), a foreign internal defence squadron and a combat weather squadron
- A **Joint Special Operations Command** (JSOC)

USSOCOM provides highly trained, rapidly deployable and regionally focused SOF personnel in support of global requirements from the national command authorities, the geographic commanders-in-chief (C-in-C) and the American ambassadors and their country teams. The Geographic C-in-C's area of responsibility (AOR) is divided into various commands. In 1999, SOF had units deployed all over the world – in 152 countries and territories (not including classified missions or special access programmes). In any given week, some 5,000 SOF are deployed in sixty countries. The characteristics of SOF personnel are shaped by the requirements of their missions and include foreign language capabilities, regional orientation, specialised equipment, training and an understanding of the political context of the mission.

Spectacular underwater view of USN SEALs with an Underwater Delivery Vehicle (UDV) of which the USN has some fifteen, which are carried in special 'Dry-Deck Shelters'. The latest UDVs can carry up to eight SEALs.
(USSOCOM)

the US Embassy compound in Tehran, was the culmination of the period of SOF decline in the 1970s and led directly to the US Defense Department creating a joint counter-terrorist task force and the Special Operations Advisory Panel. Many years of hard work and re-education followed, until on 16 April 1987, the Department of Defense activated USSOCOM. The greatest challenge was to make the Command the driving force behind the revitalisation of SOF which the US Congress had ordered, without alienating conventional military leaders and to do so against the

US Army Special Operations Command (USASOC)

Activated on 1 December 1989 and commanded by a lieutenant-general, **USASOC** is the Army component of USSOCOM. It controls:

- five active and two Army National Guard (ARNG) special forces groups totalling fifteen active and six ARNG battalions
- one active ranger regiment (75th) with three battalions
- an active special operations aviation regiment (160th) with a detachment in Puerto Rico

US ARNG SF roping down from their helicopter at the start of an operation. (USSOCOM)

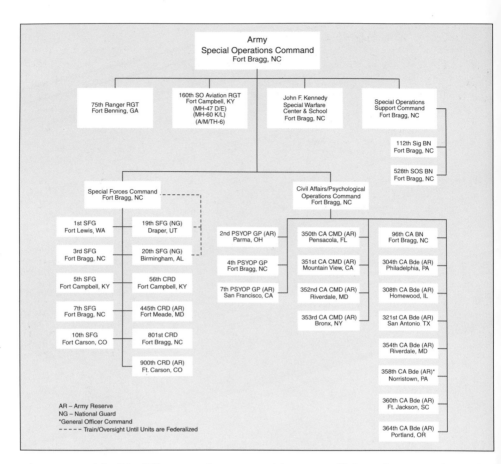

Army
Special Operations Command
Fort Bragg, NC

- 75th Ranger RGT, Fort Benning, GA
- 160th SO Aviation RGT, Fort Campbell, KY (MH-47 D/E) (MH-60 K/L) (A/M/TH-6)
- John F. Kennedy Special Warfare Center & School, Fort Bragg, NC
- Special Operations Support Command, Fort Bragg, NC
  - 112th Sig BN, Fort Bragg, NC
  - 528th SOS BN, Fort Bragg, NC

Special Forces Command, Fort Bragg, NC

- 1st SFG, Fort Lewis, WA
- 3rd SFG, Fort Bragg, NC
- 5th SFG, Fort Campbell, KY
- 7th SFG, Fort Bragg, NC
- 10th SFG, Fort Carson, CO
- 19th SFG (NG), Draper, UT
- 20th SFG (NG), Birmingham, AL
- 56th CRD, Fort Campbell, KY
- 445th CRD (AR), Fort Meade, MD
- 801st CRD, Fort Bragg, NC
- 900th CRD (AR), Ft. Carson, CO

Civil Affairs/Psychological Operations Command, Fort Bragg, NC

- 2nd PSYOP GP (AR), Parma, OH
- 4th PSYOP GP, Fort Bragg, NC
- 7th PSYOP GP (AR), San Francisco, CA
- 350th CA CMD (AR), Pensacola, FL
- 351st CA CMD (AR), Mountain View, CA
- 352nd CA CMD (AR), Riverdale, MD
- 353rd CA CMD (AR), Bronx, NY
- 96th CA BN, Fort Bragg, NC
- 304th CA Bde (AR), Philadelphia, PA
- 308th CA Bde (AR), Homewood, IL
- 321st CA Bde (AR), San Antonio TX
- 354th CA Bde (AR), Riverdale, MD
- 358th CA Bde (AR)*, Norristown, PA
- 360th CA Bde (AR), Ft. Jackson, SC
- 364th CA Bde (AR), Portland, OR

AR – Army Reserve
NG – National Guard
*General Officer Command
- - - - - Train/Oversight Until Units are Federalized

- four reserve civil affairs (CA) commands, seven reserve CA brigades, and one active and twenty-four reserve CA battalions
- one active and two reserve PSYOP groups totalling five active and eight reserve PSYOP battalions
- one active special operations support command composed of one special operations signal battalion (112th), one special operations support battalion (528th) and six special operations theatre support elements
- two active and two reserve chemical reconnaissance detachments (CRD)
- the John F Kennedy Special Warfare Center and School

The main tasks of the special forces groups, the Green Berets are, when directed, to deploy and conduct unconventional warfare, foreign internal defence, special reconnaissance and direct action missions in support of US national policy objectives within the designated areas of responsibility. Their motto is *De oppresso liber* ('Freedom from oppression'). The twelve-man Operations Detachment 'A' – usually known simply as the 'A Team' – is the key operating element of the group and five 'A' Teams are commanded by the 'B Team' which comprises six officers (including the major commanding) and eighteen men. All Green Berets must be qualified airborne soldiers, whilst some will be trained in free-fall parachuting and/or amphibious activities; all the other ranks must have at least two other qualifications, such as engineering, intelligence, weapons, signals, demolitions, languages, etc. – the usual gamut of skills so essential to be immediately available in every special forces unit.

USSOCOM Equipment

As well as using current inservice vehicles like the HMMWV and weapons such as the M16A2 assault rifle and Mini 14 assault rifle, the USSOCOM is always looking to the future and has a number of key programmes that will provide the necessary items for special forces. As far as its ground forces are concerned, examples of these new acquisitions are:

- ground mobility – a new light strike vehicle (LSV) to provide a highly mobile, rugged platform to support the five primary missions (special reconnaissance, direct action, unconventional warfare, foreign internal defence and combating terrorism) and one secondary (personnel recovery). It must have better mobility than HMMWV, carry and fire crew-served weapons, provide for a 3000 lb payload/ten-day mission, be air-transportable, have space for four to six crew, an operating range of

Of all the world's special forces **1st Special Forces Operational Detachment** – Delta or the 'D' Boys – must rank as one of the finest and most professional. It was formed officially on 19 November 1977, the brainchild of Colonel Charlie A. Beckwith, their founder and first CO, who had served on an exchange posting with the British SAS in the early 1960s. When he returned to the US, he managed to get permission to form a unit on the same lines as the SAS. Most of the US Army hold them in awe, often merely referring to them as the 'operators' or 'the dreaded D'. Delta was formed strictly for use outside the USA, and then,

supposedly, only with permission of the host country. Its likely missions are covert reconnaissance, hostage-rescue, snatching wanted men and explosive ordnance disposal (EOD). Like the SAS it usually operates in four-man teams.

The volunteer soldiers of the three battalions of **75th Ranger Regiment** are the masters of special light infantry operations. The missions of its 1,600 personnel include attacks to temporarily seize and secure key objectives and other light infantry operations requiring unique capabilities. Like their SF counterparts, Rangers can infiltrate an area by land, sea or air to conduct direct-action operations. Providing a responsible strike force and fighting primarily at night, Rangers rely on the elements of surprise, teamwork and basic soldiering skills, to plan and conduct special missions in support of US policy and objectives. They have taken part in every major combat operation in which the USA has been involved since the end of the Vietnam War, including Grenada, Panama, Iraq, Haiti and the Balkans.

The Regiment comprises three battalions, each with three combat companies of three rifle platoons and a support weapons platoon. Rangers are recruited from within the US Army, volunteers first attending a special eight-week induction course at the US Army Ranger School. Only about a third of the candidates pass this gruelling course which includes all the usual SF skills, such as land navigation, weapons handling, unarmed combat, patrolling, survival etc. This is followed by further training in mountain and jungle and swamp warfare. Exercises take place all over the USA and elsewhere in order to

Medevac by air has drastically reduced fatalities amongst battle casualties. Here a USAF medic treats a casualty before he is loaded onto a waiting helicopter. (USSOCOM)

give would-be Rangers training in as wide a variety of locales as possible. At the end, the now much smaller number of volunteers win the right to wear the black beret and Ranger cap badge, together with the 'Ranger' flash on their right arm. They will stay with the Rangers for at least two years and can extend, but only with their commanding officer's recommendation. They use standard US Army weapons and equipment.

The **160th Special Operations Aviation Regiment**, the 'Night Stalkers', provides support to SOF personnel on a worldwide basis, with their specially modified state-of-the-art helicopters, enabling them to perform a wide range of missions, including force insertion and extraction, aerial security, armed attack, electronic warfare, and command and control support. These soldiers' ability and performance exemplify their motto, 'Night Stalkers don't quit'. The 160th also provides assistance to NAVSPECWARCOM for maritime operations such as protecting oil-rigs. Current equipment includes:

- MH-47 D/E Chinook – used for medium-range night and bad-weather infiltration/exfiltration, resupply operations in hostile areas, selected rescue and recovery missions, and to refuel aircraft. There are presently twenty-five of the latest MH-47Es in service; this is the modified CH-47D Chinook helicopter.
- MH-60 K/L Blackhawk – used for medium-range, night and bad-weather infiltration/exfiltration, resupply operations in hostile areas, selected rescue and recovery missions and medical evacuation. This is the SOF version of the Sikorsky UH-60. Twenty-three MH-60Ks are currently in service.
- A/MH-6 Little Bird – used to conduct and support short-range infiltration/exfiltration, resupply in hostile

areas, selected personnel recovery missions, provide surgical point and small area target destruction/neutralisation with provision for close-air support. It includes shipboard, platform, over-water and urban operations. Forty MELBs (Mission Enhanced Little Birds) are to be procured during year 2000.

The **John F Kennedy Special Warfare Center and School** has a two-fold mission: developing doctrine and providing training courses for Army special forces, civil affairs, psychological operations and foreign area officers, and survival, evasion, resistance and escape training.

Naval Special Warfare Command (NAVSPECWARCOM)

Naval special warfare (NSW) forces are organised to support naval and joint special operations within the theatre of unified command. The forces are organised, equipped and trained to be highly mobile and quickly deployable. NAVSPECWARCOM headquarters, which was commissioned on 16 April 1987, controls:

- two active NSW groups
- five active NSW units stationed overseas
- two active special boat squadrons
- thirteen active patrol coastal ships
- three active special boat units
- two active sea-air-land (SEAL) delivery vehicle (SDV) teams
- six active SEAL teams
- The Naval Special Warfare Development Group
- The Naval Special Warfare Center

Each special warfare group has three SEAL teams, one SDV and one special boat squadron assigned.

An Air Force combat weather team in action. They are launching a weather balloon. (USSOCOM)

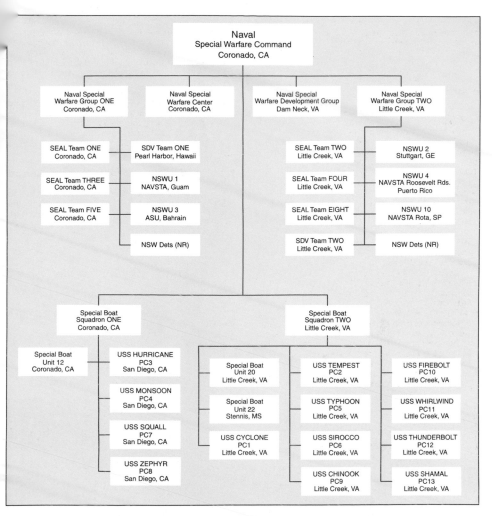

SEAL teams are maritime, multipurpose combat forces, organised, trained and equipped to conduct a variety of special operations missions in all operational environments. Operating mainly in sixteen-man platoons from sea-based platforms, SEALs primarily conduct clandestine ground and waterborne reconnaissance, in maritime, littoral or riverine environments in support of joint and fleet operations. Their history goes back to the Second World War, when in 1942, the US Navy raised a small detachment known as the Navy Combat Demolition Unit to deal with maritime and beach obstacles. Their first mission took place on 11 November 1942 during the Operation *Torch* landings in North Africa. Other teams were active in 'island-hopping' operations in the Pacific and underwater demolition teams (UDTs) cleared the beaches during the Normandy landings. Most UDTs were disbanded after the war. The small number remaining took part in the Korean War, but it was President John F. Kennedy who officially commissioned them on 1 January 1962.

The Vietnam War saw the size and scope of UDT operations increased, one estimate being that they successfully completed over 150 major missions and accounted for some 2,000 Vietcong killed or captured. Gradually the UDTs became SEAL teams, taking part in such operations as *Just Cause* in Grenada in 1983. Then in 1989, they captured Panama City airport and two years later were the first Allied troops into Kuwait City during the Gulf War.

SEAL delivery vehicle (SDV) teams are made up of specially trained SEALs and support personnel, who operate and maintain SDVs and dry-dock shelters (DDS). SDVs are wet submersibles designed to conduct clandestine reconnaissance, direct-action and passenger-delivery missions in maritime environments. DDS deliver SDVs and specially trained forces from modified submarines. SDV and DDS platoons provide the most clandestine maritime delivery capability in the world.

Special boat (SB) squadrons and units are composed of specially trained naval personnel who are responsible for operating and maintaining a variety of special operations ships and craft, such as rigid inflatable boats and patrol coastal ships, to conduct coastal and riverine interdiction to support naval and joint special operations. These specialised units have great strategic mobility and can respond to crises worldwide. They provide the Navy's only riverine operations capability and small-craft support for SOF.

Volunteers for the SEALs come only from the male personnel of the US Navy (rank is unimportant) and, once selected for training (they must be US citizens, under twenty-eight, with an IQ of 104 or higher, pass a basic fitness test, have a positive mental attitude and a clear record), they attend a twenty-six-week induction course at the Naval Warfare Center, Coronado, California. The first phase lasts for six weeks and consists of physical training and indoctrination (the sixth week is known as 'Hell Week' and is an ultimate test of mental and physical motivation); the second phase is seven weeks of more physical and endurance training, also combat SCUBA training including long underwater dives training to become basic combat divers, but always using swimming and diving to get to their combat objective.

The third phase lasts for nine weeks and covers demolition, reconnaissance and warfare on land, but with continuing physical training. The final four weeks are spent on San Clemente Island putting into practice all they have learnt. Then, in order to become fully fledged SEALs, they must pass a three-week basic

parachute training course at the Army airborne school. Posting to one of the SEAL teams follows, where, after completing six months' probation, they will be awarded a SEAL Naval Enlisted Classification (NEC) and the Naval Special Warfare Breast Insignia, known as 'the Trident'.

They are now fully fledged members of SEAL teams, each of which is generally made up of a HQ and ten platoons, further divided into two squads each of an officer and seven men. The squad consists of two four-member combat groups, each of two two-man teams. All SEAL teams have a similar organisation, but at least one team specialises in counter-terrorism operations.

Air Force Special Operations Command (AFSOC)

Established on 22 May 1990, **AFSOC** is America's specialised air power, capable of delivering special operations combat power 'anytime anywhere'. AFSOC has about 10,000 men, with some 22 per cent stationed overseas. They are highly trained, rapidly deployable airmen who are equipped with the highly specialised fixed- and rotary-wing aircraft necessary to provide SOF mobility, forward presence and engagement, precision employment/strike and information operations. The following active Air National Guard (ANG) and Air Force Reserve units are assigned to it:

• 16th Special Operations Wing (SOW) with eight special operations squadrons – five fixed-wing, one

Two US Navy SEALs make a striking silhouette against the surf. (USSOCOM)

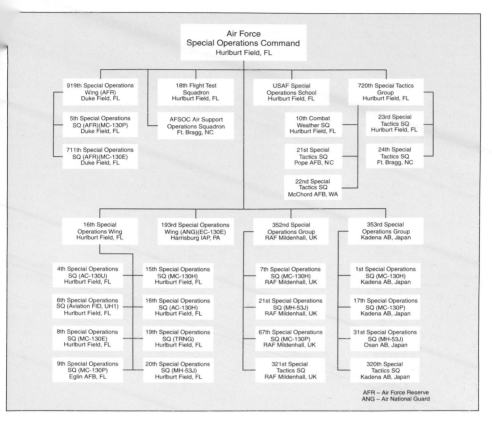

rotary-wing, an aviation foreign internal defence (FID) unit and a fixed-wing training squadron
- 352nd & 353rd Special Operations Groups, based in the UK and Japan respectively – each theatre-orientated group is comprised of two fixed-wing and one rotary-wing special operations squadron, plus a special tactics squadron
- 919th AF Reserve Special Operations Wing with two fixed-wing special operations squadrons
- 193rd Special Operations Wing (ANG) with one fixed-wing special operations squadron
- 720th Special Tactics Group
- 18th Flight Test Squadron
- the Air Force Special Operations School

The **16th Special Operations Wing** is the oldest and most seasoned unit in AFSOC. It deploys with specially trained and equipped forces from each service, working as a team to support national security objectives. The Wing focuses on unconventional warfare, including counter-insurgency and psychological operations during low-intensity conflicts. It also provides precise, reliable and timely support to SOF worldwide. Their squadrons contain a mix of aircraft.

The **720th Special Tactics Group** has special operations combat controllers and pararescue men who work jointly in special tactics teams. Their mission includes air traffic control for establishing air assault landing zones, close air support for strike aircraft and gunship missions, establishing casualty-collecting stations and providing trauma care for injured personnel.

The **Special Operations School** provides special-operations-related education to personnel from all branches of the Department of Defense, governmental agencies and allied nations. Subjects covered include regional affairs and cross-cultural communications, anti-terrorism awareness, revolutionary warfare and psychological operations.

Joint Special Operations Command (JSOC)
JSOC was established in 1980. It is a joint headquarters designed to study special operations requirements and techniques, ensure interoperability and equipment standardisation, plan and conduct special operations exercises and training, and develop joint special operations tactics.

The United States Marine Corps (USMC)
Whilst the **USMC** is not a part of US Special Forces Command, some specialist members of this massive force of nearly 175,000 active and 40,000 reserve marines, which is organised into four divisions and four wings of aircraft, deserve mention here in view of the specialist operations which they undertake and the specialist training they receive, both of which are almost identical to those of the US Special Operations Forces. Since 1775, US marines – or 'Leathernecks' as they are more popularly called – have been involved in

almost all American military activities and have earned an enviable record for their fighting prowess. They are a vital part of America's Rapid Deployment Force and have always been considered to be an elite force.

The USMC divisions (three active and one reserve) are organised, armed and equipped on the same triangular basis as the US Army, namely three infantry regiments each of three battalions (USMC units normally have some 20 per cent more manpower than their Army equivalents). Supporting troops within the division include artillery, tanks, armoured amphibians, etc. Marine aircraft wings each have about 300 aircraft – fighters, transport and tanker, observation and reconnaissance aircraft, including both fixed-wing and rotary-wing.

Within this formidable force are specialists, such as:

• Marine force reconnaissance (in US parlance 'recon') units
• Marine long-range reconnaissance battalions (LRRP)
• search and target acquisition platoons (normally one per USMC regiment)
• fleet radio reconnaissance platoons (one Atlantic and one Pacific)
• air-naval gunfire liaison companies (ANGLICO)
• fleet anti-terrorism security teams (to provide swift, short-term, professional protection on a worldwide basis, as and when needed)

Members of such units must undergo similar training to SOF personnel, so that they can undertake their missions by land, sea and air, including, for example, parachuting and SCUBA diving.

Each active marine division maintains **reconnaissance battalion** for tactical reconnaissance and a **force reconnaissance company**. The latter contains four platoons and three direct-action platoons. The seven platoons each consist of sixteen marines, divided into four four-man patrols. As they have to be the eyes and ears of the division they must be expert in aerial infiltration (HALO and HAHO) and SCUBA diving. Considered to be the 'elite' of the USMC, they can volunteer only after three to four years in the Corps and after qualifying on a specialised course (e.g. for selected marksmen) or being a member of a specialised unit such as the Scout Sniper Platoon (SSP). They must also pass the Army airborne test which includes running three miles in eighteen minutes, swimming 500 m, retrieving a heavy object from the bottom of a swimming pool and completing a testing obstacle course in under five minutes. Following an interview they then go on to form part of the Recon Indoctrination Platoon (RIP) to complete their training. Later they attend the School of Amphibious Reconnaissance and have to pass a three-week diving course, followed by a month of parachuting.

The standards are exceptionally high, only two or three out of the original sixty being eventually selected. Following their posting to a unit they will complete their training which will include courses at Survival, Escape, Recon and Evasion (SERE) School, Scout Sniper School (SSS) and jungle environment survival training (JEST). A chosen few may also be integrated into Delta Force (Army) or Team 6 (Marines).

The CV-22 Osprey is a variant of the USMC MV-22 tilt-rotor aircraft (seen here) which will be able to carry out long-range, night and bad weather infiltrations/extractions/resupply for SF missions. It has vertical/short take-off and landing ability (V/STOL) and some fifty are to be procured. (Bell Boeing)

The Sikorsky UH-MH 60 Blackhawk helicopter, as seen here on a ship's flight deck, is one of the most widely used SF helicopters in the world. It can carry eleven passengers in addition to its three-man crew. (USSOCOM)

Rapidly becoming the fast attack helicopter of the decade, the McDonnell Douglas AH-64 Apache is due to enter service in the British Army this year. It is of course in service with the US forces. This version – the AH-64D Longbow Apache, has the distinctive radome which can penetrate rain, fog and smoke, plus its sixteen Hellfire missiles and 30 mm chain gun. The British models are being built by GKN Westland. (GKN Westland)

Police Forces of the World – Specialised Teams

The Nationella Insatsstyrkan (NI) *is the Stockholm Police's national Intervention Unit for all Sweden. Two of their assaulters are seen here in full gear with night-viewing devices, radios, etc. The photo also shows their arm badges very well.*
(Stockholm Police)

As well as the Special Forces found within many of the world's military forces, many of the world's police forces now have their own specialised teams which they have formed in order to deal with all manner of illegal activities such as hostage taking, drug dealing and other forms of global terrorism, organised crime and the like. Some of these have already been mentioned in the main text where they are so linked with the particular country's SOF as to make it difficult to separate them. Whilst these are not strictly 'Special Operations Forces' within the military meaning of the phrase, they are highly trained, lavishly equipped and operate much as SOF do – albeit usually on a more limited scale. And furthermore, it has to be said, they are probably individually far more well trained in SOF skills than many of their military counterparts. Therefore, they still need to be covered in this guide. These units include the following, but please appreciate that this list is not exhaustive and there are probably many others not listed. However, it does give some indication of the serious way in which most countries in the world now take the increasing need for SOF to tackle global criminals. In the cause of brevity, I have included only a representative 'smattering' of the special weapons and equipment as used by these teams, however, it goes without saying that most use very similar weapons and equipment, 'black Nomex' clothing with hoods and bullet-proof vests, being the universal 'dress of the day' for these remarkable modern-day, elite warriors.

Australia

Australia's specialised police units include the **Australian Protective Service (APS)** and the **VIP Protection Australian Federal Police Hostage Rescue Unit**.

Austria

A police commando unit, known as *Gendarmeriekommando Bad Voslau* (after the name of its home base) was formed in 1973 as a result of a wave of terrorist incidents in Austria. Five years later it was reorganised and became **Gendarmerie Einsatz Kommando (GEK)** Cobra. Its success has led to other countries forming similar 'Cobra' units.

ABOVE: *Good close-up of* Gendarmerie Einsatz Kommando *(GEK) Cobra with an AUG 9 para submachine-gun which is a conversion of the Steyr AUG assault rifle. Its sight gives remarkable accuracy out to 200 m. (Steyr Mannlicher AG & Co KG)*

BELOW: *Two members of GEK Cobra leaving a stream. The leading one is carrying an AUG 5.56 mm assault rifle which is known by the Austrians as the* Sturmgewehr 77. *It is also widely used by other law enforcement agencies. (Steyr Mannlicher AG & Co KG)*

Belgium

The **Escadron Spécial d'Intervention (ESI)** of the *Gendarme Royal* was formed in 1972 as a result of terrorist attacks like the one on the Israeli athletes at the Munich Olympic Games (see Germany). It was known initially by the codename *Le Groupe Diane* – it changed its name to the ESI two years later, but is still called 'Diane' in the Belgian press. Those serving in the ESI are all volunteers and their selection and subsequent training as rigorous as all other SF forces, however, unlike most other Western SF forces, the ESI allows women to serve in the unit (but only in observation and undercover roles). As well as anti-terrorism duties they can be called upon to act against drug dealers and armed criminals, indeed much more of their time is now spent dealing with organised crime than with counter-terrorist duties.

Canada

The **Special Emergency Response Team (SERT)** of the Royal Canadian Mounted Police (RCMP) is organised, trained and equipped along similar lines to the other permanent anti-terrorist assault forces maintained in other countries, like the GSG9 in Germany and the GEK (Cobra) unit in Austria. Based in the National Capital Region and reporting to the Deputy Commissioner, Criminal Operations at HQ RCMP, it will respond to incidents which happen anywhere in Canada. The Canadian Armed Forces will assist as and when necessary, in particular with the provision of specialised transportation (e.g. helicopters or armoured vehicles). SERT has a strength of forty-nine (two groups of twenty-four, plus a commander) and one group is kept at constant readiness, the other

on 'instant recall'. They can, when necessary, respond as one group, and/or receive extra manpower from one of thirty-one Emergency Response Teams (ERT) stationed across Canada which have a total manpower of some 350. Volunteers for this unit must have served a minimum of eight years in the RCMP, be approximately thirty-two years old and have a high performance assessment. They were originally drawn from ERT members, narrowed down first to ninety. Future SERT members now attend a nine-day selection/screening process and, if chosen, serve for three years with the SERT before re-integrating with their former duties in the RCMP. Training includes extensive hostage rescue techniques, which were learnt from the British SAS. SERT team members carry gasmasks, and wear tight black hoods and bullet proof vests. Earpiece-type radios, stun grenades, commando knives, H&K SMGs and SIG-Sauer automatic pistols, rapelling ropes and hooks, flashlights, etc., are standard equipment and weigh about 20 lb, but do not restrict movement in any way. And of course in addition to this standard equipment, there is the usual arsenal of other weapons (e.g. tear gas guns and sniper rifles with nightscopes), mountaineering equipment, and even a four-man battering ram, is available! 'Money well spent' is how the RCMP Commissioner views the $11 million which has been spent setting up SERT, which has certainly taken much of the risk out of potential hostage situations and other emergencies.

Colombia

The **Grupos Especiales des Operaciones (GEOS)** of the National Police Force is a GSG9-type unit (see Germany).

In the good old days all the Mountie needed to 'Get his man' was his trusty steed, pistol, red jacket and funny hat. Now the RCMP Special Emergency Response Team (SERT) requires more modern gear, as this excellent 'old and new' photograph shows. (Gilles Rivet/Concord Publications)

Czechoslovakia

Utvar Rychleho Nasazeni **(URNA)** is the Czech Special Police anti-terrorist unit. Located in barracks some 75 km from Prague and created in the early 1980s, this rapid response unit is designed to deal with terrorists, kidnappers, hijackers, drug traffickers and other organised crime. URNA consists of three groups, an administrative group (to cover logistics and the inevitable paperwork), a special services group (specialists such as snipers and negotiators) and an operations group. The last of these consists of some eighty-five police officers divided into three assault teams whose mission is to carry out high-risk arrests, so they include experts at getting into buildings, various forms of transport etc., using mechanical or explosive means. Each team also has men who are qualified in EOD. All are trained in skin and SCUDA diving, rescuing people from aircraft, trains and metros etc., with special training facilities available to represent such scenarios.

Denmark

Politiets Efterretningstejeneste **(PE)** is part of the State Police Intelligence Service.

Egypt

Force 777, a highly secret counter-terrorist unit, has been dealt with already in the main text as its composition (military/police?) is not accurately known.

Finland

Osasto Karhu – 'The Bear Unit' of the Helsinki police department – is a counter-terrorist unit.

France

RAID (nicknamed 'The Black Panthers') is a counter-terrorist organisation and, like so many other similar organisations worldwide, its men dress all in black when on operations and it is generally very secretive. Formed in 1985, they are one of the few SF who recruit direct from the general public. They have a strength of some sixty operatives, divided into four ten-man teams, with an HQ and support group (10) and a specialist group (also 10) who handle negotiations, etc.

Groupe de intervention gendarmerie nationale **(GIGN)** is the French police counter-terrorist unit, formed in 1974. It recruits exclusively from the ranks of the *Gendarmerie* and to be eligible a volunteer needs five years' experience with an exemplary record, however only some 7 per cent of those who apply are accepted. Ten months' of intensive training follows before joining one of the four fifteen-man groups which make up GIGN, together with a command and support group and a special negotiation cell – total strength is about ninety. GIGN operates all over the world and in many different environments. Since its formation it has taken part in hundreds of operations, freed many hostages and 'eliminated' dozens of terrorists. One of its recent successes was the release of 173 passengers and the shooting dead of four Algerian Islamic extremists who had hijacked an Air France airbus in Algiers, which they forced to fly to Marseilles on 26 December 1994 after killing three hostages. The extremists had planned to fly on to Paris and crash the plane, but were thwarted by GIGN action.

Germany

Grenzschutzgruppe **9 (GSG9)** is the para-military arm of the German police which came into existence after the Arab 'Black September' terrorists broke into the Olympic Village near Munich on 5 September 1972, killing some Israeli athletes and taking others hostage. A rescue attempt at the Furstenfeld military airport by the German police went tragically wrong and during the gun battle all nine hostages were killed, as were four Arab terrorists and a policeman. Three Arabs were captured and one escaped into nearby woods. As a result of this débâcle, GSG9 was formed and proved itself five years later, when on 18 October 1977, they stormed a Lufthansa airliner at Mogadishu airport, killing three of the four Palestinian terrorists and freeing all the hostages unharmed, just one hour before the terrorists' deadline for blowing up the plane and its eighty-six passengers expired. Members of the British SAS were reputed to have been part of the GSG9 assault team.

Not recommended for amateurs! Not the easiest way to travel by helicopter, but when needs must then hang on tight! (GSG9)

The highly successful GSG9 has become a 'role model' for a number of other police counter-terrorism units worldwide. GSG9 operatives have also given advice/assistance to other similar anti-terrorist units during particularly difficult operations. Members are all volunteers, either from the border police or the Army, and must undergo an arduous course, lasting nearly six months and covering both strenuous 'SAS-style' training as well as police duties and legal matters, indeed considerable emphasis is placed upon such academic matters as well as the physical side. The failure rate is high with only some 20 per cent being selected. GSG9 use the H&K MP5 9 mm submachine-gun which is one of the most widely-used weapons of its type in this field, despite being more complex and considerably more expensive than most other SMGs. It has a number of variants (e.g. A2 has a fixed stock, A3 a telescopic metal stock, MP5K a short-barrel being designed for ease of concealment, MP5 SD incorporating a built-in silencer). Pistols favoured include the Walther P5 and P88; the H&K P7, P9 and P9S.

Organisation. GSG9 has an establishment strength of 238, although their actual strength is currently only

Members of Grenzschutzgruppe 9 (GSG9), one of the most efficient and able of the police counter-terrorist organisations, are seen here with a display of some of their weapons, equipment and means of transportation. One can quickly see why the maintenance of such a force is so expensive. (GSG9)

180. It is divided as follows:

Commander GSG9
Operations Staff
External Advisors and Technical Support Staff (incl. medical)
Combat Units

1. GSG9	2. GSG9	3. GSG9	4. GSG9
conventional comprising: machine-gnrs, riflemen (incl. sniper)	maritime specialists trained in naval special warfare (trained by elite naval commando divers)	para trained in HALO and free-fall parachuting	as for 1.

A group of GSG9 policemen show off some of their devastating firepower, which includes a wide range of Heckler & Koch weapons. (GSG9)

As with some of the cantons of neighbouring Switzerland, various German *Laender* have their own 'special insertion commando', including Baden-Wuerttemberg and Bavaria. GSG9 and these *Spezialeinsatzkommando* work very closely with the special police forces of the various cantons (see Swiss entry for details).

Greece

Dimoria Eidikon Apostolon **(DEA)** is a special mission platoon of the Athens police with counter-terrorist duties.

Holland

Brigade Speciale Beveiligingsopdrachten **(BSB)** – literally 'Unit for Special Security Assignments' – is a part of the Dutch 'Royal Mounted Police' **(Koninklijke Marechaussee)**, which has responsibility for guarding the frontiers of the Netherlands. BSB duties include providing security at Schiphol International Airport.

OPPOSITE: *Hostage rescue from hijacked aircraft remains one of the GSG9's most important and difficult tasks. (GSG9)*

Hungary

The **Police Special Force (PSF)** is a counter-terrorist organisation.

India

The **National Security Guards (NSG) Special Action Group** and **Special Rangers Group** are both a mixture of police and military. They are a large force, one recent estimate being 7,000, and are used for counter-terrorist operations. They have been used on numerous occasions, for example in 1984 and 1986, when the Sikh militants were besieged in the Golden Temple at Amritsar.

The Special Protection group specialises in guarding VIPs.

Indonesia

Indonesia's specialised police units include the **Police Mobile Brigade** and *Satgas Gegania* (Counter-Terrorist Task Force) of the Indonesian National Police.

Israel

Police Border Guards, also called the 'Green Police' operate in anti-terrorist and special operations within the borders of Israel and its occupied territories. They have already been covered in the main text on Israeli SOF, as have YAMAM and YAMAS, which are SOF units of the Israeli National Police Corps.

Italy

Italy is a country in which the criminal activities of the Mafia clans together with terrorist groups like the Red Brigade, have led to many situations that have required resolution by special assault squads beyond normal police capabilities. This led to the formation of **Nucleo Operativo Centrale di Sicurezza (NOCS)** – the Central Operative Group for Security – whose successes have included the release of US General James L. Dozier from the Red Brigade in 1982. Since their formation they have participated in a staggering 5,000 missions, including 400 security and Judicial Police operations and about 200 high risk arrests. There are about 100 officers in the NOCS (compared with some 80,000 officers in the Italian Police Corps) and they are divided into assault squads capable, for example, of freeing hostages, carrying out assault operations in both urban and rural settings, providing support for other police departments that need a specially trained group to ensure the success of an operation, and protection of VIPs both inside Italy and abroad. Weapons used include Italian-made Beretta 9 mm pistols, Beretta M12 9 mm SMGs, Beretta AR70 assault rifles, SPAS 12 shotguns, and Beretta AR70 and AR70/90 assault rifles, as well as foreign-produced weapons. They are also one of the few police assault groups that use armoured face masks capable of withstanding projectiles fired by small-calibre weapons.

Gruppo d'Intervento Speciale (GIS) is a 100- strong volunteer force which stems from the *Carabinieri* and was raised in 1978 to fight the Mafia, the Red Brigade and similar criminal organisations. Entry tests are extremely hard and at least 40 per cent fail. This is followed by a two-week selection process, then a ten-month course for those selected, which includes combat shooting and driving (the latter supposedly on the Ferrari road circuit). One of their recent operations was the storming of the belltower in St Mark's Square in Venice, which had been occupied by separatists demanding an independent northern state, in May 1997. They use much the same weaponry as the NOCS.

Japan

Police action units.

Jordan

The police operate a national SWAT team known as **Unit 14**, which comes under the jurisdiction of the Public Security Department. Its main task is anti-drug interception, although it can be used jointly with SOU 71 (see main text).

Kenya

General Service Units (GSU) of the Kenya Police.

Malaysia

The Royal Malaysian Police have two special units, **Unit Indak Khas** (Special Action Unit) and **Unit Timpan Khas** (Special Strike Unit).

Mexico

Force F of the Mexico City Police are used in counter-terrorist and hostage situations, in addition to other police work such as drug-related crime. As one might expect, their nickname is 'The Zorros'!

Morocco

Gruppe Intervention Gendarme Nationale (GIGN) is a counter-terrorist group.

New Zealand

New Zealand has special police heavy weapons tactical teams.

Norway

Beredskaptroppen of the National Police is a counter-terrorist group formed in 1975. This all-volunteer force recruits only from serving Norwegian policemen with two years' unblemished service. They have operators who are parachute trained and HALO qualified, whilst others qualify as SCUBA divers. They have their own fleet of all-terrain vehicles as well as Volvo cars (940 Turbos), and also can call upon military helicopters or naval craft as necessary. The force works closely with other Scandinavian police forces and the military.

Philippines

Light Reaction Force of the Philippines Constabulary Integrated National Police Field Force.

Portugal

Grupo de Operacoes Especials (GOE) is the Portuguese counter-terrorist and hostage rescue unit.

It is part of the national police and trained by the British SAS with whom they maintain strong ties – as they do with the Spanish GEO. The Portuguese GOE was yet another counter-terrorist unit formed in the wake of the rise of world terrorism in the 1970s and 1980s. They have a high reputation as being one of the best intervention squads in the world. Under the Command HQ, the force is divided into four main groups: Special Intervention Unit; Operations and Communications; Command and Support; and Administration. They have 'on call' a wide range of all types of transport, military and police helicopters and naval vessels.

Singapore

Police Tactical Team

South Africa

The **Special Task Force** of the South African Police is similar to the GSG9.

Spain

The Spanish National Police Corps has a special anti-terrorist corps assault group called the *Grupos Especiale de Operaciones* (GEO), which is designed for assault and capture operations requiring highly trained personnel using special techniques. It was started in November 1977, when Captain Ernesto Romero drew up a report on Spain's specific needs in this field. Approval was given to form the force and some 400 serving police officers volunteered. After a series of

Members of Grupos Especiale de Operaciones (GEO), *the Spanish National Police Forces anti-terrorist group, are higly trained and have plenty of experience with ETA and similar terrorist organisations. Here a party of GEO officers use a modified off-road vehicle with a roof structure that allows the installation of various lengths of ladder to reach difficult areas quickly.* (GEO)

Stun grenades explode as this GEO team practises assaulting buildings. (GEO)

detailed tests, as directed by Captains Ernesto Garcia-Quijada and Juan Senso Galan, some seventy were chosen then reduced to fill the fifty positions available. Training then took place at a barracks belonging to the Armed Police Force of Guadaljara, in subjects such as weapons handling, physical training, personal defence, parachuting, swimming and explosives. The first course ended on 19 January 1979 and subsequent courses have continued ever since. Since 1979, GEO has participated in hostage rescues, aeroplane hijackings, drug trafficking etc., the most significant activities being against the radical Basque organisation ETA. They have also worked abroad, providing security to Spanish diplomats and served as special instructors to Guinea, Ecuador, Algeria, Mexico and Egypt. To date more than 400 officers have joined GEO, only some 10 per cent of the original applicants of each intake passing out, so the training is tough and demanding. Weapons used include the inevitable H&K MP5 SMG, 12 bore shotguns, pistols, and sniper rifles. In the past year, the GEO has received additional equipment in the shape of new helmets, new tactical combat vests, leg holsters for the new SIG Sauer P226 steel pistols with optional laser sights and built-in flashlights, and the 5.56 mm calibre SIG assault rifle.

GEO organisation. Under the command of the Commissioner of Police and based in Guadalajara, some 50 km from Madrid, the GEO is divided into two sections, the Operations Section and the Support Section. The former consists of the following Operational Groups: three Operational Action Groups which are commanded by Chief Inspectors/Inspectors and divided into three Subgroups led by subinspectors and composed of two commandos of five men each. Each man in the commando has a special skill: two snipers, one breacher, one diver and one special systems expert. Next is the training and Specialities Operational Group of about ten men. They are responsible for giving the specialist courses for all GEO volunteers, all those courses for foreign units

Emerging from the water with his H&K MP5A2 SMG at the ready, this GEO officer presents a fantastic picture. (GEO)

and, most importantly, they also carry out periodic resits and retraining of the operators and support the Operational Action Groups in their daily training. The final group is the Techniques and Experiences Operational Group, again composed of some ten men. They carry out studies and tests of new material, develop new techniques and operational procedures,

The H&K MP5 SMGs are fitted with Sure-Fire flashlights on the handguard and visible or IR lasers at the front. (GEO)

make reports on possible targets and follow and analyse critical incidents which have occurred in other countries. The Support Section is in charge of managing all the Unit's equipment and provides logistic, administrative and technical support. Personnel in this section man such locations as vehicle-gun workshops, offices, communications, medical and health, stores and security, etc.

GEO attaches great importance to planning joint training with foreign units worldwide, whilst giving courses to such countries as Mexico, Ecuador, Honduras, Guinea, Algeria and Egypt.

The other small specialist counter-terrorism unit of the *Guarda Civil* is the elite **Unidad Especial de Intervencion (UEI)** with some fifty members, which is responsible for dealing with foreign terrorists who may commit violent acts on Spanish soil. In addition, they are also committed to combating the Basque separatist movement. Formed in 1982, from *Guarda Civil* volunteers, they normally wear police uniform but when on operations invariably wear black Nomex coveralls.

Sweden

Stockholm's County Police Authority has a National Intervention unit – **Nationella Insatsstyrkan** (NI) – a counter-terrorism unit some fifty strong, broken down into teams which can cover all aspects of a terrorist situation, including negotiation and assault, as well as intelligence gathering, individual sniping, command and control etc. It is also used for drug raids, VIP close protection, high risk warrants and other risky operations throughout Sweden. The County Commissioner is the final arbiter in deciding whether or not the unit will be deployed in a terrorist action in Sweden. The use of weapons follows the regular rules for police using firearms. Responsibility for Crisis (Hostage) Negotiation rests with the Commander NI.

Switzerland

Detachment Enzian (Det E) is a special unit of the Bern Canton Police which deals with anti terrorist/special operations. Named after the hardy little Alpine flower (also known as the Gentian) which grows in the mountains of Switzerland, they have built up a formidable reputation over the past three decades. They were founded in 1972 by *Oberst* Hans Arnet, commandant of the Canton Police, after the Palestinian Black September atrocities in the Olympic village in Munich. Although the Bern region has been relatively free from terrorist attacks for the past twenty years, Det E is always ready 'just in case'. In 1994, they were amalgamated with the Criminal Police section to form an autonomous special force, fully capable of dealing with violent criminals as well as terrorists. They have also had to provide numerous VIP escorts for such visitors as the Pope, HM Queen Elizabeth II, Yasser Arafat, and the American Defense Minister, William J. Perry. Their tough selection process sets them apart from the rest of the police force and leaves them well prepared to combat the most hardened thugs in the most dangerous areas. Det E contains some thirty men, all volunteers, all highly trained and ready to be used as a last resort in any emergency.

Other cantons have also formed their equivalent special police units, for example:

Canton	Name of force	Date formed	Remarks
Vaud	Le 'Dard'	1991	*Détachement d'Action Rapide et de Dissuasion* – 31 members (incl. 9 dog handlers)
Aargau	'Argus'	1975	Contains 37 members
Zurich	'Diamant'	1993	Approx. 70 members
Solthurn	'Falk'	1977	25–30 members (incl. 7 snipers)
Neuchatel	Le 'Cougar'	1976	*'Courage, Organisation, Unité, Groupe d'Action Rapide'* Organised into 15 units
Basel-Stadt	'Basilisk'	1979	Approx. 50 members
Basel-Land	'Barrakuda'	1994	26 members
Fribourg	Le 'Grif'	1988	*Le Groupe d'Intervention de la Police Cantonale Fribourgeoise*
Tessin	Ticinesi sono bravi agenti di Polizia	1978	22 members

Tunisia

Groupement de Commando of the Garde National (GCGN).

Turkey

Jandara National Police SWAT Teams.

United Kingdom

The London Metropolitan Police **D-11** unit is similar to the GSG9. They also have three other special units: **SO 19** – Force Tactical Firearms Unit; **SO 11** – Metropolitan Police Surveillance Unit and **SO 10** – Witness Protection Unit.

United States of America

Specialised police units in the USA include: **FBI Hostage Rescue Teams (HRT)**; the **Nuclear Emergency Search Team (NEST)** of the Department of Energy; **Treasury Enforcement Agents (TEA)** in Special Response Teams, assigned from the headquarters in Washington of the Bureau of Alcohol, Tobacco and Firearms of the Treasury Department; and secret service agents who protect the President.

Various police departments within the USA have their own Special Response Teams, for example the Phoenix, Arizona, Police Department Special Response Team and the Special Operations section of Atlanta, Georgia. Both are fully equipped with all possible means of carrying out their duties, which include assault and arrest operations. In Phoenix, the small group of officers comprises the **Special Assignments Unit (SAU)** which, since its establishment in 1961, has provided specially chosen, trained and equipped forces to handle police situations beyond the scope of the regular force.

The **Special Operations Section** of Atlanta can deploy SWAT (Special Weapons and Tactics) teams, who are protected by heavy, bulletproof shields and safety gear, and are trained to deal with snipers, bomb deactivation etc. and have to do so on at least fifty calls a year. There are two squadrons of Special Operations personnel and each SWAT team has within its ranks three individuals who specialise as snipers (one of whom is female) and six as bomb deactivators.

New York's 'finest' the NYPD have an **Emergency Service Unit** – a 400-man SWAT and rescue force. The men and women of this elite force are trained in all the normal SF skills, so there are commandos, SCUBA-divers, medics and snipers. Their task is probably more difficult than that of similar units in the other US cities because they must protect world leaders *en masse*, when they gather at the United Nations Plaza in New York.

Body Armour

Body Armour. An essential part of SF equipment in life-threatening situations is body armour of one type of another. It is designed to protect only the most vulnerable parts of the body (e.g. chest and back) because an 'all-over suit' as needed for bomb disposal, would be far too cumbersome for most SF operations. Invariably body armour is worn with black Nomex clothing and respirators.

Body armour will stop most low velocity attacks at 5 m and has been in service with both British and US SF since the mid-1980s. (All photographs in this section copyright 'Armour Shield')

Index